Starting Out

Starting Out

ESSENTIAL
STEPS
TO YOUR
DREAM
CAREER

PHILIPPA LAMB AND NIGEL CASSIDY

BBC
BOOKS

Published by BBC Books, BBC Worldwide Limited,
Woodlands, 80 Wood Lane, London W12 0TT

First published 2004.
ISBN 0 563 52140 6

Commissioning Editor: Emma Shackleton
Project Editor: Mari Roberts
Designer: Ann Thompson
Production Controller: Christopher Tinker

Set in Frutiger
Printed and bound in Great Britain by Mackays of Chatham

In memory of Justin Crawford.
A man who worked hard to build
a happy life – and succeeded.

Contents

'Life is short but it sure feels long if you're in a boring job.'

Anonymous

Chapter 1
Why read this book?

In this chapter you will find:

❏ How to take the first step towards finding work that does more for you than just pay the bills

❏ How to get the best out of this book

Wondering what to do for a living? Or maybe you haven't even thought about it because you've been so wrapped up in working out which subjects you want to take at school or college or dealing with university. Either way, you need to think about how you want to spend your working life, and this book is here to get you started. Whatever sort of job you end up doing it's going to take up a huge amount of your time and energy, so it's important that you enjoy it. *Starting Out* is the first step towards finding work that will do far more for you – and your happiness – than just pay the bills.

Putting aside time now to think about how you might like to earn a living instead of rushing into a decision later will be one of the best moves you ever make. The work you do will have an enormous impact on almost every aspect of your life. We're not just talking about how much you will earn, but also where you are likely to live, the people you will meet and the amount of free time you will have for things like friends, family, travel or sport.

Whatever age you are and whatever education choices you still have to make, if you are thinking about careers, *Starting Out* should help you get on the right road.

By reading this book you will begin to equip yourself with the self-knowledge you need to work out what sort of job will satisfy and challenge you. Combine that with the good grounding you'll get on the practical realities of working life in the 21st century and you should be heading in the right direction, instead of stumbling around not knowing where to start.

Still not convinced? Well, if you're still wondering whether to read this book or not, how about taking another look at the quotation that appears on the previous page?

■ So what are you going to do with the rest of your life?

Feel like a laugh? Enter the word 'careers' into a search engine. Ours took just 0.14 seconds to come up with 15,900,000 suggestions. How helpful is that? Not very, when you come to think about it.

As you will soon discover, one of the biggest problems you're going to run into when it comes to researching careers is the sheer volume of information that's out there – there's just too much.

But don't panic. You don't need to worry about all that yet. This is the book you need to read before you even start getting bogged down in all that careers stuff in the library, let alone the internet. This book is not just about career planning; it's about work and life and working life, and how to make your work fit with the life you want.

If you stopped ten people in the street and asked them to name a great job they'd probably come up with things like these:

TV presenter
top-flight lawyer
pop star
chief of a big, successful company
brain surgeon
vet
supermodel
professional sportsman or woman
film star
travel journalist

And there's no question that these can (note the word 'can') be great jobs to do or aspire to, but it's a very limited list and most people don't end up doing any one of them. You may be one of the few who do, but before you decide to head off down one of those roads, you should take a look at what else is out there because there's a whole string of other jobs that are likely to be as good a fit for you – if not better.

Wherever we live, and often without us realizing it, our career ambitions are heavily influenced by the society we live in and by rapidly shifting fashions. Here's a fascinating example of what that means in terms of you and the work you might end up doing. In Japan, becoming a professor is one of the top dream jobs for boys, while running a restaurant or food shop is the most popular career choice for girls. In India, working in banking is a top choice among young people of both sexes.

Now think about that for a moment. Young people in Japan and India aren't fundamentally any different from you. Chances are most of them want pretty much the same things you do – a fulfilling and happy life with enough money to do and buy the things they want. But how many twenty-somethings in Britain would put 'becoming an academic' down on a list of dream jobs? Or running a food shop or working in a bank?

The point we're trying to make here is that you need to question where your ideas about which jobs are desirable are coming from. Are they yours, or have you absorbed them from your parents, friends or the media? If you're going to put in all the time and effort it takes to build a great career, you want to be sure you've chosen one that you're genuinely suited to.

Advice from parents, relations, teachers and friends is usually well meant and often helpful but you don't necessarily have to follow it. This book will help you sort out the facts about work from the fiction, and show you how to put your own ideas about work to the test.

■ Why plan your career?

Planning your career is important because the chances are you will need to move several or even many times as your working life progresses. This can be a difficult idea to get your head round. There you are wondering what particular work might suit you, and already we're telling you that you might have to move on. It's a fact that the old idea of doing 'a job for life' has gone for good. For most of us, 'a life of jobs' is probably a better description of what lies ahead.

Don't worry. With the help of this book, you can start tackling it one simple step at a time. And managing your career isn't rocket science – more a question of learning to build up a bank of skills and experience to carry you from one stage to the next.

As an adult you're going to spend more than a third of your waking hours at work – and it could end up being a lot more. This book is here to maximize your chances of enjoying that time as much as possible. It will:

■ Help you to find out more about who you are, what motivates you and what you want out of life. Understand yourself and you can get a better idea of the work you'd find challenging and rewarding.

- Tell you what working life is really like. Your friends, family and teachers all have their own ideas about work and you've been absorbing images about jobs from books and the media for years. Learn to separate fact from fiction.
- Show you what employers want from their staff. Their wish-list is changing – and as future employees you need to know what's on it.
- Explain how working life will change in the future. If you know what's round the corner you can plan for it.
- Give you the tips you need to help you successfully manage your career. After all, do you really want to leave something this central to your happiness to look after itself?

Once you've digested that lot, you should find that thinking about careers starts to feel like something you might like to do, as opposed to a task you don't want to face. So forget about grabbing leaflets at random from the careers library, and turn that computer off for a while. If you're sick of feeling confused about which subjects to pick or whether to stay in education, or just fed up with trying to work out what to do with your life, all you need right now is this book.

■ Why *now* is the time to make a start

Very few people wake up one morning with a clear idea about what they want to do for a living. And even fewer systematically make all the right choices to lead them to that dream job.

Nowadays career planning comes a long way behind coursework, exam preparation and the seemingly endless choices you need to make about subject options, GCSE subjects and college or university entrance. In many ways, that's as it should be. You should keep your options open as long as possible – because you'll probably change your mind about careers again and again. But in the end the system forces you to narrow down your choices, so – whatever stage you're at in your education – you do need to start thinking about the possibilities that are open to you and the longer-term implications of the decisions you're making.

▇ It's your life – so take control of it

If working life still seems too far off to worry about, try thinking about it this way: unless you win the national lottery (in a rollover week when you're the only person with the winning numbers), you are likely to spend at least 40 years of your life working (and there's a good chance it could be more like 50). Now imagine getting up every morning, week after week, for all those years, to go and do a job you don't enjoy.

That's how life is for millions of working people because they ended up in jobs they never planned to do. They drifted from school to university, college or work without really thinking about what they were doing, and chose a job purely because it happened to be available or paid a better salary than anything else they were offered at the time. If you don't want to find yourself in that situation, you need to start thinking objectively about who you are and what is important to you; and learning as much as you can about the working world that's about to open up to you.

▇ How to get the best out of this book
'Even a mosquito doesn't get a slap on the back
until it starts to work.' Anonymous

First the good news: there is no need to read this book from cover to cover, starting with the introduction and ending with the final chapter. Once you've read this chapter, the order in which you read the rest of the book is completely up to you. You've got other things to do and we've deliberately designed *Starting Out* so you can dip into it when you have time.

For example, if you've got half an hour to spare and you feel like stretching your brain a bit, then Chapter 8 would be a good place to go. You'll learn some seriously useful 'big picture' stuff about how work fits into the national economy and how the jobs on offer are changing rapidly.

But if all that information seems a bit heavy-duty for the mood you're in, then how about getting together with a mate for a bit of self-analysis? In that case, try Chapter 3 and do some of the quizzes together to find out more about who you are and what sort of work might suit you.

Basically it's up to you. If you take our advice you'll make sure that you've read the whole book at least once by the time you finish your education, but how long it takes you to do that is your business.

Enjoy …

My five dream jobs:

1. NME journalist, 1976–1979

2. Producer, Atlantic Records, 1964–1971

3. Any kind of musician (apart from classical or rap)

4. Film director (although preferably not German or silent)

5. Architect (I used to be quite good at technical drawing at school)

Adapted from *High Fidelity* by Nick Hornby

Chapter 2
So you want to be a ...?

In this chapter you will find:

❏ Why many young people decide they like or dislike certain jobs without knowing enough about them

❏ How to work out where the ideas you already have about jobs have come from and whether you can rely on them

❏ Why well-meant advice from parents, friends and teachers may not always be in your best interests

How many jobs can you name? That might sound like a stupid question, but why not give it a try? Take five minutes and see how many different jobs you can write down on a sheet of paper. Now run down your list and tick the ones you actually know something about (and by 'something' we mean a bit more than just 'Accountant – sorts out people's tax', or 'Policewoman – catches criminals').

If you've managed to come up with 10 or 15 jobs that you genuinely have more than a passing knowledge of, you've done well. But think what a tiny fraction these represent of all the jobs you might possibly do nowadays.

So how do you work out which ones you might like to do? There are countless careers you could pursue – and probably a good many jobs that you think you might like to do. As we'll explain later in the book, the best way to start tracking down the ones that would suit you best is to start amassing more information about:

- Your personality and abilities
- What you want out of life
- What different jobs involve
- How working life operates now and how it's likely to change in the future

Later in the book we'll show you where you can start to look for the information you need – and how to use it to help you start planning your future. First, though, it's worth taking a long, hard look at the ideas you already have about work and working life.

■ Look before you leap

What makes certain jobs more appealing to you than others? Where do your perceptions about them come from, and should you be relying on them? If you want to feel confident about the career decisions you make, then you need to spend some time working out the answers to these questions and thinking about how realistic your ideas about particular careers are.

Statistically, most teenagers have some idea about what they think they want to do by the time they're 17. Having said that, there is no need to panic if you are already 16 or 17 and haven't reached any conclusions. It might feel as if you are the only person who still hasn't made their mind up, but that won't be the case. You should not feel pressured to opt for a particular career path if you're not sure it's the right thing for you. There's nothing wrong with being uncertain, it just means that you haven't got enough information on which to base a sound decision.

If this is you, the first step is to work out exactly what sort of information you need to get your hands on. For example, you may feel that you know where your personal strengths and weaknesses lie but not be sure which careers might suit you. If that's your situation, then Chapter 6 should help get you started.

On the other hand, you may already have identified jobs that appeal to you but be unclear about whether you're suited to do them, or how to go about pursuing them. In that case, the Connexions website should help (see page 219). It features a vast range of jobs and contains a mass of information about what each one involves and the educational and personal attributes you will need to do them.

Even if you leave school or college still uncertain about the path you want to take, there's no need to worry. More and more people do a range of different types of work during the course of their lives nowadays, and just because you start your career in one job doesn't mean you can't rethink and move into something completely different a year or two down the line.

■ The jobs we think we want

What *is* a bad idea is turning your back on all sorts of potential career avenues without really knowing what the work involves. Right now, while you may feel very warm about certain jobs, you probably also have a hard-bitten prejudice against others. It's a fact that we rule out most careers by the time we are 11. Yet at this age, how could we possibly know what these jobs are like? Just where are our ideas coming from?

So, if you don't want to cut yourself off from the full range of opportunities open to you, it's time to confront any preconceptions and prejudices you might have about particular jobs. We all have them, and much of this chapter is about helping you to understand what yours are and where they came from. In the late 1990s, some academics at Southampton University (Foskett and Hemsley-Brown 1997) carried out a research study to try to find out what schoolchildren thought about different jobs. They talked to young people aged 10, 15 and 17 living in various parts of the country and they discovered some interesting things.

The most popular jobs were in the arts and media

This includes acting, TV presentation and journalism – with 18 per cent of young people overall saying they wanted to work in these areas. If you're one of them, you might like to bear in mind that the number of people studying journalism in the UK is now believed to be slightly higher than the number of people currently earning their living as journalists. This is not to say that you shouldn't pursue a career in the arts or media, but do the maths first. Even with the expansion of the media sector, there just aren't enough jobs available to absorb all those students, so a good number of them will end up doing something else.

Younger children were particularly keen on the idea of working with animals or in the arts and media (particularly the girls) or sport (particularly the boys)

But their ideas obviously changed over time because the study found that older children were more focused on the professions: medicine being the first choice for 18 per cent of them, followed by arts and media (15 per cent) and financial services (11 per cent).

Children from different social classes had different aspirations

Those from lower-income backgrounds liked the idea of doing something in sport or joining the armed forces, while middle-class children were aiming for medicine and management.

Needless to say, no single study can tell the whole story and it would be foolish to generalize too broadly about class issues. Enormous numbers of young people go on to establish impressive and lucrative careers without having had the advantage of an affluent family background. Similarly, a middle-class home is no guarantee of career success. The point we're trying to make here is that when we are young, our ideas about work tend to conform to those of the people we spend most of our time with.

This brings us to something else you will need to keep in mind from now on. It's that influential people around you, like family, friends and teachers, also have their own set of personal experiences, preferences and prejudices which may colour the advice they give you. They all want to help, but you will need to weigh up what they're saying as objectively as possible.

To reach an informed choice, you will have to sift out the facts and opinions you can rely on from ill-informed (even if entirely well intentioned) suggestions. Remember – it's your career, not theirs.

■ What do most people want to do?

Following the crowd is no way to pick a career but if you're curious about what other teenagers are doing you can check out the most popular degree and HND courses on the UCAS website (www.UCAS.ac.uk) to get an idea of what's popular in the UK right now. Of the 273,000 students who graduated in 2003, 80 per cent studied one of the following ten subjects (in order of popularity):

business and administrative studies
creative arts and design
social studies
biological sciences
subjects allied to medicine
languages
engineering and technology
computer science
history and philosophical studies
physical science

In the 2002/3 year, applications were markedly up for:

law
psychology
medicine (and the 2004 applications were even higher)
sports science
media studies
dance
forensic science

But although these subjects are still popular, interest seems to be fading slightly at present in:

computer science
electronic and electrical engineering
veterinary science

As for what undergraduates are planning to do with their degrees, this 2003 survey from the Careers Research and Advisory Centre shows the sort of work that 1,000 of them were hoping to do when they graduated. They were asked which area they would like to work in for their first job. The results are interesting. Twelve times as many graduates were interested in working in sales than in science, for example.

WHAT UNDERGRADUATES WANT

Management 17%	Publishing 4%
Banking and financial services 13%	Charity 3%
Sales and marketing 12%	Education 3%
Other 9%	Hospitality and tourism 3%
Consultancy 8%	Public service 3%
IT 6%	Environment 2%
Engineering 5%	Construction 1%
HR 5%	Science 1%
Law 4%	Social health care 1%

■ The jobs we think are not for us

One thing we should all be wary of is leaping to conclusions about which people in life are suitable for which jobs. Almost 30 years after Britain first passed sex equality laws, the majority of jobs are still being done mostly by men or mostly by women. Yet that's no reason for you to feel that certain jobs are not for you purely because of who you are.

According to the Equal Opportunities Commission, three-quarters of working women are still employed in just five areas:

administration and secretarial work

personal services, such as caring for children or elderly people

sales and customer service

associate professional and technical work, such as nursing

non-skilled manual work

This is not good news, because jobs seen as 'women's work' are generally lower paid than 'men's work', even where they require similar qualification levels. Women who work full time take home on average just over 70 per cent of a man's annual salary for the same job. If the pay gap continues to narrow as slowly as it has done for the past few years, researchers from the Fawcett Society estimate it could take another 85 years for it to close completely. They blame the gap on discrimination and the number of women who work in low-paid or undervalued occupations.

So-called 'sticky floors' trap women in menial jobs and 'glass ceilings' block women's progress up the career ladder, and they are still a reality in the workplace. However, the gap does tend to be narrower in the service sector and the professions.

■ Diversity matters

So much for sex discrimination, but women aren't the only ones having a tough time in the working world. Discrimination on all sorts of other grounds undeniably remains commonplace but – and it's an important 'but' – it's less common than it was. Laws are now in place to protect all of us from being treated less favourably by potential employers or at work on a wide range of grounds including:

sex
race, colour, nationality, ethnic origin
disability
faith
sexual orientation
and, in 2006, age as well

What this means is that there is no reason why you should accept any career limitations on these grounds. If you run up against discrimination, then use the law and stand up for your rights. If you don't, you become part of the problem instead of part of the solution.

Generally employers are keen to show that they want a 'balanced' workforce including people of all types and backgrounds, but many complain that they find it hard to attract workers from minority groups. Recruiting women and older workers doesn't tend to be a big problem, but one in five of the organizations that took part in a CBI survey said they found it difficult to attract applications from people with disabilities and from ethnic minorities. Importantly, they say one of the big reasons for this is that potential staff falling into those categories are often reluctant to apply because they think that particular jobs or employers are 'not for them'.

It's clear from this that employers are still not yet doing enough to make their organizations into the sort of places where everyone would feel welcome and comfortable. But it also means that you need to be careful not to write off potential jobs based on preconceived ideas you might have about them or the attitudes of an organization that is advertising vacancies.

According to the CBI's research, banking, finance, insurance, transport and communication, distribution, hotels and restaurants are the sectors most likely to encourage applications from diverse backgrounds. Don't take that too literally, though. The situation varies enormously from employer to employer, and you shouldn't be put off a sector just because it doesn't appear in that particular piece of research.

◼ Employment and social class

The days when jobs were allocated on the basis of your social class or position in local society are largely gone. At the top of the tree, working-class board directors are no longer a rarity. As for the shop floor, if you took a random sample of people doing what might be classified as a 'low level' job, like shelf stacking in a supermarket, you might be surprised at the social diversity you would find.

People of all ages and backgrounds now do all sort of jobs. The reasons for their choices may range from pure economic necessity (due to divorce, bereavement, family break-up, the need to finance further education, etc.) to language or cultural barriers preventing people from doing work for which they are otherwise qualified. Then there are considerations such as the need to find work that fits in with childcare or looking after sick or elderly family members.

◼ Commitment *vs* qualifications

Yet while prejudice in all its forms is alive and well among British bosses (and their staff), it may be possible, on occasion, to turn belonging to an 'underrepresented' group to your advantage when you're job-hunting. According to the Chartered Institute of Personnel and Development, some employers are so keen to have a more diverse workforce that they are offering jobs to people from minority groups even if they don't have all the necessary skills or experience to do the work from day one. The only requirement is that they have the necessary potential. That's well worth bearing in mind if you think you might fall into a category of people that employers are keen to see on their staff.

It could mean that if you're thinking of applying for a job but you're not sure that your CV is strong enough, it's still worth going for it. If you can convince them that your commitment will make up for your lack of qualifications, you might stand a better chance than you think.

◼ Time for a reality check

There is absolutely nothing wrong with being ambitious about the sort of job you'd like to do. Aim as high as you like – but make sure you also keep your feet on the ground. The research team from Southampton University found that one in every five 17-year-olds they talked to was aiming for a high-profile, highly paid job such as professional sportsman or woman, actor or TV newsreader. These are sometimes known as 'lottery jobs'. Like winning the lottery, the possibility of you actually getting one owes a lot to chance – being talent-spotted, for example, or happening to meet someone who thinks you would be perfect.

So what's the obvious message here? If you think about it, not even one in every thousand teenagers is going to end up with a lottery job. You might feel certain you will be the one in a thousand – and you might be right. But if you are thinking along these lines, it might be time to make a cool assessment of your talents and abilities – and of the levels of competition you are likely to face.

Unsurprisingly, as teenagers get older, most – though not all – become more realistic about their job prospects. But just where do we get all our ideas from in the first place?

■ Playing doctors and nurses

In the same way that advertising shapes our ideas about what we should buy and where we want to live, TV programmes, news coverage, newspapers, magazines and books influence our views about work.

Take gender – we all know that, with a few legal exceptions such as Catholic priests, the vast majority of jobs are now open to both men and women. Yet we still may be subconsciously limiting our options based on out-dated stereotypes. Why on earth, for example, do some people think there's something remotely unusual about women becoming builders or men working as receptionists? Fortunately, ethnic, gender and age-related stereotyping is less common now than in the past, but it's still around, and some of the pre-conceptions people have about different jobs probably stem from things they read or saw as a child.

When it comes to how we view the working world, television pro-grammes and films are hugely influential. Teachers say they know what was on TV the night before by the games children play in school. The visual media undoubtedly shapes how appealing we find particular jobs. Research shows, for example, that many of the opinions young people have about nursing as a career are formed from watching programmes such as *Casualty*, *Holby City* and *ER*.

As a result, the most attractive medical jobs are perceived to be ambulance staff or doctors in accident and emergency departments. Nurses are viewed much more negatively as 'helpers' who work for the doctors (which, of course, they don't – increasing numbers of nurses are becoming practitioners in their own right).

The same goes for jobs in the law. Around the time of the O.J. Simpson murder trial in the United States, career guidance staff found that teenagers suddenly became fascinated with the idea of training to be a barrister. More recently, university admissions tutors and recruiters for law firms report that some applicants tell them their interest in the law first came from watching *Ally McBeal* when they were younger.

The way police work is dramatized on TV doesn't seem to be helping recruitment into the main police services, but interest in working in criminology, forensics and psychology is rising, thanks to the exciting way such work is portrayed in programmes like *CSI* and *Cracker*.

Yet how true to life are such TV programmes and films? Do we really believe most pathologists spend their time running around playing detective like Amanda Burton in *Silent Witness*? (Mind you, if you do, you're not alone – applications to this field shot up by over a quarter in 2003, and more than 80 per cent of the people who visit the *Silent Witness* website say they'd like to work in forensics.)

Jobs in vogue change from year to year. At the moment, career guidance professionals report a lot of interest in roles such as:

TV presenter
lawyer
doctor
pharmacist
interior designer
property developer
physiotherapist

If you count up all the celebrity-based competitions, legal and medical dramas and shows focusing on how to make money from property on TV currently, you'll soon see why certain jobs are considered hot. Would you believe the popularity of physiotherapy is partly put down to the possibility it brings of working with sports celebrities? Imagine that – a whole career based on the chance that you might spend half an hour massaging Michael Owens's shin or Thierry Henri's hamstring.

Just because law and medicine are very popular right now is no reason to avoid those careers if you think they'd suit you and you believe you have what it takes to succeed in a competitive and academically demanding field. But you already know that fiction and real life are two different things – so don't fall into the trap of thinking that the careers you see on screen and read about in books bear much relation to reality.

■ Jobs are not always what they seem

It's not just the media that can provide us with a misleading picture of working life. In the course of our day-to-day lives we all build images in our minds of what it would be like to do various jobs. Often they're based on the short periods of contact we have with people, whether they are shop assistants, bank staff, doctors, nurses, estate agents, dinner ladies, vets, refuse collectors, mechanics or whatever occupation we come into contact with.

We see jobs being done for a brief period of time – in the case of service providers such as shop assistants it can be just a few minutes. Yet we instantly make assumptions about the job and about them. Some of those assumptions will be correct. For instance, it's fair to assume that if you decided to work in a shop, you'd spend a lot of time sitting or standing behind a till. If you became a refuse collector, you could count on having to be out in all weathers.

However, other assumptions wouldn't be correct. Shop staff, for example, might order or choose stock, take deliveries, sort, mark and display goods, deal with banking and administration and spend time helping customers on the phone as well as in person. And the job they are doing might be the first rung on a training programme that leads to a more rewarding job in the organization. Many retailers require new management trainees to work initially on the shop floor. Just because you see or know about certain aspects of a job doesn't mean you are getting an accurate picture of the whole thing.

Studies suggest that many young people especially like the idea of 'helping' as part of their work. The Southampton study we mentioned earlier found that teaching, medicine or becoming a vet are seen as more appealing than working in the law, business, finance, engineering or science.

Yet *all* these careers involve using expertise to provide clients with specialized help or solutions. It goes to show how important it is to find out what jobs actually involve rather than what you think they involve. For example, you might think finance is only suitable for people who are motivated by money, but everyone needs sound financial advice to be able to make the best of the income or investments they have. Charities and the public sector draw on the skills of large numbers of finance people. There are thousands of organizations doing valuable work overseas and at home – from providing famine relief to low-cost housing. All of these rely on well-qualified financial staff to manage their budgets for them.

To take another example, the legal profession provides plenty of openings for those who want to make a difference to people's lives. Currently, there's a shortage of people working in the area of legal aid for clients who can't afford to pay their own legal fees. Much the same goes for engineering – think about vital aids such as prosthetic limbs for amputees and lightweight wheelchairs for children. Without input from engineers, these aids would not exist.

■ Teachers – what do they know?

Teachers also play a big part in the decisions you make about careers. They are likely to be among the first people you turn to for information and guidance. Indeed, careers teachers are there for exactly that purpose, although it's important to recognize that most of them are teachers first and careers specialists second. However, they should be helpful and enthusiastic, and might have years of experience in guiding young people's career choices.

But by the time you have dealings with your careers teacher you may have already amassed some pretty firm ideas about work and different jobs. At primary school and in the earlier years of your secondary education, you were constantly subjected to your class teachers' thoughts about careers and work. As the Southampton team point out, this means that what you know or do not know about careers, training and entry requirements is closely linked to what *they* knew (or didn't know!).

Researchers quizzed teachers in a selection of primary and secondary schools about where they got their information and knowledge about careers from. The vast majority of them said that they mostly relied on ideas they got from friends, their own personal experience, and the media.

Sound familiar?

To be fair, they must also be getting careers information from books, magazines, videos and other resources, but you should be aware that the information and advice you absorb at school may be subjective and is certainly not comprehensive.

Teachers in the study admitted that they knew far more about academic career pathways for school-leavers (i.e. higher education) than they did about vocational routes. 'Vocational training' is a catch-all phrase meaning further studies you do after your formal education which are going to be of direct help in getting or advancing in a job.

This means that the work ambitions and images they pass on to you are not necessarily up-to-date. Although they have your best interests at heart, what they know about different routes to different careers might be based largely on how things were when they were making their own career choices. The last thing you want to happen is to find yourself going in a particular direction because you never discovered what the alternative options were.

At least teachers aren't pretending to know more than they do. In the Southampton study, 70 per cent freely admitted they had 'little or no knowl-edge of the nature of careers and jobs in engineering' – not very helpful for the more science-orientated of their pupils. However, if it's accurate, objective and up-to-date information about specific jobs that you're after, the internet is ultimately the best place to go for it anyway. (See the end of the book for details of useful websites to visit.)

In short, through sheer daily exposure, you are inevitably absorbing your teachers' perceptions about work. Would you believe Foskett and his team found many teachers were not overly positive about any single career other than – you've guessed it – teaching? So at least nobody could accuse them of not doing their bit to ensure the survival of the teaching profession.

Needless to say, teachers don't set out to mislead you. They want to help. But they're only human, and just because you're happy with their ability to teach you maths or English doesn't mean you shouldn't ever question their ideas about careers.

■ Parents have seen it all before (or have they?)

In the same way that teachers make an impact on your attitudes to work because they spend long periods of time with you, your parents' ideas about careers will inevitably colour your judgement about what sort of jobs you find appealing. The most obvious example of this is your attitude to the work that your parents do. If you dad works in the NHS or your mum has a job with the local authority, you'll be on the receiving end of huge amounts of information about those jobs.

You'll also receive very strong 'delegated images' (their views passed on to you) about what it's like to do those jobs. So you'll learn a great deal, but also absorb subjective opinion about the merits or value of their work.

Many parents have strong ideas about what their offspring should do for a living. Although they would never say it publicly, careers advisers sometimes find parents more of a hindrance than a help when it comes to talking to their kids about work options.

It may be that your parents' ideas are too narrow, rigid or over-ambitious for you. It may be that they're unwilling to accept the idea that a child of theirs could want to do a job that does not appeal to them. Alternatively, it may be a job they don't know much about. This is a common problem now as there are lots of 'new' jobs around that your parents may never have heard of.

Professional parents can find it difficult to accept the idea of their child opting out of higher education and going straight into work or work-based training at 16 or 18. Similarly, teenagers from families where no one has gone on to higher education before can find themselves under pressure to leave school and get a job. At the other extreme, they could be under pressure to go to university and get the higher education their parents missed out on.

Resisting pressure of this sort can be tough – particularly if you are made to feel that you're disappointing your parents. This is usually best tackled by politely but firmly explaining the reasons for your chosen path.

Some parents are prone to thoughts of basking in your future success and do have a tendency to be 'over-directional' – that is, they have rather fixed ideas based on their own experience of the working world and may push you in the wrong direction. They may have to get used to the idea of you wanting to do something radically different, or outside their understanding.

Keeping it in the family

Parents may get upset if you don't want to join the family business. Every year hundreds of family firms are closed down or sold because nobody in the next generation wants to take them on. If you are resisting joining the family firm, do lots of research into your chosen field – and show the rest of the family what you have found out. It can be upsetting for parents to have spent a lifetime building up an enterprise only to find none of the children wants to take it on, so try to show them what is enthusing you instead.

If your parents think your career ideas are outlandish or unrealistic, don't give up. Tell them you are serious, but keeping your options open. Perhaps you could let them help you devise a Plan B to fall back on. In this way, if your grand scheme to become a Formula One driver, a dot.com millionaire or a City trader fails to materialize, you can start off in another direction.

Parents don't always behave logically or predictably. Contrary to what you might expect, they may not necessarily be happy about the idea of their children taking up the same career as them. Some will be delighted, but a parent who has been disappointed in his or her career may take a negative view of you going down the same road.

Parents may even feel threatened by the thought that your expertise and seniority in their chosen field may in time become greater than theirs. This might seem strange, but the success of a son or daughter can be a difficult thing for parents to accept. They've spent years teaching you about everything from how to use a knife and fork to why recreational drug use is not a good idea, and the thought of your respective roles ever being reversed can be hard for them to swallow.

'Helpful' relatives – handle with care

Even supportive family members can be surprisingly tricky to handle. Their ideas about what it's like to start at the bottom of the ladder in, say, IT, nursing or insurance, are almost inevitably going to be well out-of-date. Chances are it's at least 20 years since they started out and, given the pace of change in the workplace, that might as well be the Dark Ages. Your parents may not grasp the problem at first – we all like to think that we're well informed about our field and none of us likes to think that our knowledge has passed its sell-by date.

Be tactful. In terms of hard information about current routes of entry to particular jobs, such as the best universities to go to for particular courses, the entry requirements and quality of training offered by particular employers and so on, do your own research because you need to be sure you're right up-to-date. Careers advisers, older siblings and friends, and the internet, are the places to go for that. But don't discount how valuable your parents can be in terms of introducing you to useful people and giving you the inside track on what it will be like to work in your chosen career. Corporate brochures and websites are useful but their purpose is to sell you a positive image of the organizations which pay for them. If you want to know whether you'll enjoy a job or not, there's no substitute for talking to as many people as possible who are already doing it.

■ Key points

- ■ Ask yourself how much you really know about jobs and working life.
- ■ Face up to your preconceptions and prejudices about particular jobs.
- ■ Look at where your ideas are coming from – are they yours or someone else's?
- ■ Learn to sift objective advice from subjective.
- ■ Understand that this is your decision – other people can help but it's up to you to make it happen.

'Trying to define
yourself is like
trying to bite
your own teeth.'

Alan Watts

Chapter 3
Just who do you think you are?

In this chapter you will find:

❏ That like-minded people choose the same kinds of job

❏ More about your own preferences – see if you can start matching them with possible careers

❏ How organized you are

When you are slaving away at school or college, it might seem that landing a good job is entirely dependent on getting good marks in a seemingly never-ending string of exams. In fact, your own personality, values and skills will play as great a part in determining what work you are suited to as your academic or vocational qualifications.

Not so long ago, the idea of trying to find a job to suit your personality would have been seen as rather strange. Anyone without a particular career path in mind would invariably finish their education and head straight for one of the largest employers in the area. People picked somewhere jobs were available, secure and relatively easy to get to by public transport. Sons and daughters often ended up doing similar work to their mum or dad.

Life has moved on.

The idea that what work we do might be decided by where we happen to live, or what our parents did for a living, is rightly regarded as outdated. It certainly doesn't hold out the prospect of a particularly enjoyable career. Now it's recognized that our chances of future success are far higher if we first take the time to find out more about ourselves.

■ What are you like?

Each of us has a unique combination of natural strengths and weaknesses that makes us the person we are. Experts tell us that by the age of 13, many aspects of our adult personalities are already in place.

Scary, isn't it?

Your friends might have a shrewd idea what you are like – but you yourself might not have stopped to think much about your own style and behaviour.

All this is worth thinking about because different personality types do have different ideas about what a 'successful career' actually is. If you don't start off by trying to understand what makes you tick, you might find yourself trying to fall in with other people's ideas of success. What your parents or your mates might think is a great job could be totally unsuitable for you.

Some people like to think they can be a 'jack of all trades' and turn their hand to anything. It's true that versatility is increasingly important – employers love to talk about 'multi-tasking' and having adaptable workers who can apply themselves to whatever job needs doing. (For more on what employers want, see Chapter 9.) In reality, though, we all have a different combination of skills and abilities. This is not to say that only people with particular personality types are suited to a set range of jobs. There are painfully shy actors, squeamish nurses and merchant seamen who get seasick on every voyage. All we are saying here is that broad personality types are simply more likely to enjoy some roles in life than others.

To put it another way, if you analysed what kind of people tended to become carpenters, journalists or merchant bankers, you would find that many – though by no means all – would share some personality traits. So it stands to reason that the more you understand your own personality, the more your eyes will be opened to the vast array of opportunities that might especially suit you.

▓ No use faking it

Now it's true that human beings are pretty versatile. With the right training and aptitude, most of us could probably manage to do all kinds of jobs. But would we want to do them for the rest of our lives? It really is horses for courses. Take the Channel 4 documentary series *Faking It.*

One programme showed how an insurance salesman underwent extensive training and fooled a panel of experts into thinking that he was an experienced film and TV stuntman. In another, a straight-laced ex-naval officer managed to turn himself into a convincing drag queen, and a young solicitor was transformed into a club MC.

Yet, interestingly, almost every individual who took part in the series reverted to their former occupations. Almost all of them confessed some time after the series was over that they wouldn't have enjoyed their new careers on a permanent basis. So it seems the participants had probably already found their true occupations in life. With training, a gregarious risk-taker with a strong artistic streak might be capable of holding down a job as an accountant, but the chances are that he or she wouldn't have a lot of fun doing it week in, week out.

■ Feelers and thinkers

Think about your friends, or members of your family. Some people are more naturally touchy-feely than others. They have bags of compassion and they always make you feel better when you're down. Then there are the thinkers – the kind of people who can keep a cool head when decisions have to be made. But their cold logic and dislike of getting involved can be infuriating.

Clearly, those with a preference for feelings will score over the thinkers in any situation when sensitivity to other people's emotions and needs is important. However, if you were looking for someone to study some solid information and make an important decision on it, the thinker would definitely be the man or woman for the job. You can already start to imagine the different kinds of work that might best suit the feelers and the thinkers.

■ Tests can help you find out about yourself

When you start looking for jobs or applying to a particular employer, you might be asked to take tests or questionnaires designed to help build a profile of your characteristics, personality and abilities. These kinds of test come in and out of fashion and some career experts and academics disagree about how useful they are.

Even the greatest fans of testing have to acknowledge that questionnaires have their limitations. For example, while a test can suggest if a job might suit you, it cannot predict with any certainty how well you are going to perform once you have got it.

When it comes to finding work that might suit you, no test is going to help you more than a really thorough careers interview. But as long as you look upon any test as a way of finding out more about yourself and the choices you might like to explore, then you should find it helpful.

If you are keen to explore personality testing beyond the level we can cover in this book, it really is best to work with someone properly qualified to give you the most accurate results. Do take anything you find on the internet with a pinch of salt – but having said that, there are lots of websites with a range of self-tests and quizzes you can try out. You will find some of these listed near the end of the book.

QUIZ: HOW WOULD YOU DESCRIBE YOURSELF?

Look at yourself in the mirror. Describing your appearance is pretty easy. But have you ever stopped to think about how you would sum up what you are like inside as a person? What is your approach to life? What are your characteristics? Perhaps this is something you have not given much thought to – maybe now it's time you had a go.

Let's begin with a test. Don't take the results too seriously – but they should help you as you read on and start to think about the kind of work that might give you the most satisfaction. This questionnaire measures how you describe yourself. There are no right or wrong answers. There is also no time limit, but most people take about 30 minutes to complete the test. Before you start, make sure that you understand the instructions.

Here's what to do. On the left-hand side of the table, you will see a series of describing words. Taking each of the 90 words in turn, decide whether this is most like you or least like you. If you are neither one extreme nor the other, you can choose 'Neither'. Tick the column that applies to you.

The easiest way to score your results is probably to make a numbered list on a separate sheet of paper and tick (most like you), cross (least like you) or write 'N' (neither) next to each number as you go through the table.

	Most like you	Least like you	Neither
1 Calm			
2 Cynical			
3 Sociable			
4 Confident			
5 Creative			
6 Systematic			
7 Trusting			
8 Relaxed			
9 Talkative			
10 Cooperative			
11 Practical			
12 Methodical			

	Most like you	Least like you	Neither
13 Enthusiastic			
14 Imaginative			
15 Persevering			
16 Happy-go-lucky			
17 Patient			
18 Easy-going			
19 Nervous			
20 Passive			
21 Disorganized			
22 Easily upset			
23 Shy			
24 Absent-minded			
25 Challenging			
26 Emotional			
27 Undisciplined			
28 Assertive			
29 Self-sufficient			
30 Factual			
31 Reserved			
32 Accepting			
33 Precise			
34 Retiring			
35 Anxious			
36 Artistic			
37 Stable			
38 Sceptical			
39 Down-to-earth			
40 Temperamental			
41 Cold and distant			
42 Chaotic			
43 Diplomatic			
44 Composed			

	Most like you	Least like you	Neither
45 Innovative			
46 Dominant			
47 Fun-loving			
48 Detail-conscious			
49 Outgoing			
50 Pragmatic			
51 Critical			
52 Quiet			
53 Sensitive			
54 Flexible			
55 Meticulous			
56 Humane			
57 Self-assured			
58 Spontaneous			
59 Volatile			
60 Lively			
61 Open-minded			
62 Conscientious			
63 Outspoken			
64 Realistic			
65 Competitive			
66 Unruffled			
67 Rigid			
68 Confrontational			
69 Inward-looking			
70 Impulsive			
71 Tense			
72 Deep			
73 Inventive			
74 Informal			
75 Balanced			
76 Hands-on			

	Most like you	Least like you	Neither
77 Charitable			
78 Participating			
79 Exacting			
80 Tolerant			
81 Original			
82 Free-spirited			
83 Sober and serious			
84 Conceptual			
85 Theoretical			
86 Untidy			
87 Self-reliant			
88 Matter-of-fact			
89 Restless			
90 Active			

Copyright Psytech International www.psytech.co.uk.

■ How to score your answers

This takes a few minutes, so don't rush it. And it's not a simple question of the higher the score, the better!

The results are organized into five grids, which represent five key areas. When you have scored the test, your results will show how you described yourself in each key area. For example, the first one shows your degree of extraversion – the extent to which your thinking is shaped by the world around you, rather than by your inner thoughts and reflections.

To find your score, work through each of your answers in turn, circling the number in the grid here that corresponds to your response. For example, if you felt that describing word number 3 ('sociable') was 'most like you', give yourself two points. If you felt it was 'least like you', give yourself zero. If you answered neither, give yourself one point. Once you have completed each grid, add up the total score of the numbers you have circled.

1. EXTRAVERSION

Question	Most like you	Least like you	Neither	Question	Most like you	Least like you	Neither
3	2	0	1	47	2	0	1
9	2	0	1	49	2	0	1
13	2	0	1	52	0	2	1
16	2	0	1	60	2	0	1
23	0	2	1	69	0	2	1
29	0	2	1	78	2	0	1
31	0	2	1	83	0	2	1
34	0	2	1	87	0	2	1
41	0	2	1	90	2	0	1

Total:

2. OPENNESS

Question	Most like you	Least like you	Neither	Question	Most like you	Least like you	Neither
5	2	0	1	61	2	0	1
11	0	2	1	64	0	2	1
14	2	0	1	72	2	0	1
24	2	0	1	73	2	0	1
30	0	2	1	76	0	2	1
36	2	0	1	81	2	0	1
39	0	2	1	84	2	0	1
45	2	0	1	85	2	0	1
50	0	2	1	88	0	2	1

Total:

3. AGREEABLENESS

Question	Most like you	Least like you	Neither	Question	Most like you	Least like you	Neither
2	0	2	1	43	2	0	1
7	2	0	1	46	0	2	1
10	2	0	1	51	0	2	1
18	2	0	1	56	2	0	1
20	2	0	1	63	0	2	1
25	0	2	1	65	0	2	1
28	0	2	1	68	0	2	1
32	2	0	1	77	2	0	1
38	0	2	1	80	2	0	1

Total:

4. STABILITY

Question	Most like you	Least like you	Neither	Question	Most like you	Least like you	Neither
1	2	0	1	40	0	2	1
4	2	0	1	44	2	0	1
8	2	0	1	53	0	2	1
17	2	0	1	57	2	0	1
19	0	2	1	59	0	2	1
22	0	2	1	66	2	0	1
26	0	2	1	71	0	2	1
35	0	2	1	75	2	0	1
37	2	0	1	89	0	2	1

Total:

5. CONTROL

Question	Most like you	Least like you	Neither	Question	Most like you	Least like you	Neither
6	2	0	1	55	2	0	1
12	2	0	1	58	0	2	1
15	2	0	1	62	2	0	1
21	0	2	1	67	2	0	1
27	0	2	1	70	0	2	1
33	2	0	1	74	0	2	1
42	0	2	1	79	2	0	1
48	2	0	1	82	0	2	1
54	0	2	1	86	0	2	1

Total:

■ How to interpret your answers

Once you have a total score for each category, you can read off your results from the tables below. All you need to know is that:

0–11 is a low score in that category

12–24 is an average score in that category

25–36 is a high score in that category

Let's see how you fared in each of the five categories.

1. EXTRAVERSION

If you are a **low scorer** you are happy to work independently, away from the distraction of other people. You enjoy your own company and have little need for constant contact with others. It is likely that you will take a while to get to know new people and may slip into the background at social events. You are unlikely to require constant variety, change and excitement. You may prefer roles that involve independent work and not constantly having to meet and deal with new people.

If you are a **high scorer** you greatly enjoy the company of others. Talkative, outgoing and sociable, you dislike being on your own for long periods of time. By nature lively and participative, you enjoy social occasions and are likely to take centre stage at parties and events. You actively seek variety and change and need a high level of stimulation in order to avoid becoming bored. As a result, you may prefer roles that involve a high level of social contact, particularly if this involves initiating, developing and maintaining relationships.

2. OPENNESS

Low scorers are down-to-earth people who have their feet firmly planted on the ground. Your thinking style is realistic and practical and you are inclined to reject theoretical approaches to problem-solving. You will be more interested in learning practical skills and techniques that have immediate relevance. Preferring to focus on concrete issues, you will be more concerned to get things working than to ponder why they work. As a result, you are likely to enjoy roles that involve solving real-life problems.

High scorers are inclined to think in abstract theoretical ways. At times you may become so involved with your own thoughts and ideas that you lose track of practical realities. Being open to theoretical possibilities and unconventional ideas, you are inclined to bring a radical, innovative approach to problem-solving. You are likely to enjoy roles that provide opportunities for you to express your creativity and originality in a scientific, artistic or business context.

3. AGREEABLENESS

Low scorers are especially suited to roles where it is important to have a cool and questioning take on other people's behaviour. You are likely to be a little cynical, suspicious or sceptical, and may sometimes question other people's motives. As a result you will not easily be taken in by flattery or praise. With practice, you may be able to train yourself to be less suspicious.

High scorers are trusting and kind-hearted by nature. You are quick to help those you see as being more needy than yourself and are inclined to give people the benefit of the doubt. However, others may sometimes take advantage of your goodwill. You are a good team player, suited to all roles that require building trusting relationships with others.

4. STABILITY

Low scorers are prone to mood swings and can be volatile, which can make life interesting at times. You may be easily upset by others or react badly to criticism, even if it is valid. You may have a tendency to worry about past failures. Stressful work is not likely to suit you, nor might working long hours under pressure.

High scorers are emotionally stable, calm and composed, and not prone to mood swings. You generally cope well under pressure, and are unlikely to become tense, irritable, moody or upset by what others say. You could be well suited to roles that are emotionally challenging or involve working under pressure for long hours.

5. CONTROL

Low scorers tend to be spontaneous and impulsive, and comfortable with change. You are suited to roles that require adaptability and flexibility, and don't enjoy making detailed plans and schedules. You are unlikely to be particularly well organized or systematic in your work, and must guard against losing interest in tasks before they are finished. You may spread yourself across too many different jobs at once. You might be ill-suited to roles that involve rigidly following set systems, procedures and rules.

High scorers on this scale pay attention to detail and display self-control and restraint. You are well organized, and like to plan ahead carefully. Diligent and persevering by nature, you have a strong sense of duty. Once you have started a task, you are likely to feel compelled to see it through to the end. You feel comfortable working in well-structured environments. You might not be best suited to working in places with rapidly changing priorities and goals, where you have to constantly think on your feet.

So, how accurate were your results? Did they help you start thinking about the kind of roles you might enjoy? Whatever the outcome, it's worth remembering there are no right or wrong answers, and it might be that you came out some-where in the middle in some of the categories. Alternatively, if you got a very high or low score in each of the five, it could be that you were cheating! But if it gave you a taste for more self-analysis, read on.

QUIZ: WHAT TYPE OF PERSONALITY ARE YOU?

There are lots of ways specialists try to measure personality. One of the best known involves trying to match people with one or other of 16 personality types. This is in line with research by three pioneers in this field: Carl Jung, Isabel Meyers Briggs and her mother Katharine C. Briggs.

In this section we're going to have a look at what those types are, and you can decide which you think might best describe you. It's all based on the theory that everyone has a dominant style of behaviour within four categories.

These are:

1. *Where our energy comes from*
2. *How we take in information*
3. *How we like to make decisions*
4. *The basic lifestyle we prefer*

Taking each in turn, the theory is that we tend towards either:

1. *Extraversion or Introversion*
2. *Sensing or INtuitive*
3. *Thinking or Feeling*
4. *Judging or Perceiving*

Don't worry if you don't understand what these mean – their meanings should become clear as you read on.

As you can see, an initial letter stands for each tendency, and what you will end up with is a four-letter description of yourself. So, what are the four categories, and which do you think might apply to you? Just for fun, let's start to find out.

1. WHERE DOES YOUR ENERGY COME FROM?

We are all two-faced. One of our faces looks out to other people, activities and things. That's our *extraverted* face. The other looks inside to our thoughts, interests and imagination – the *introverted* face. Most of us get our energy from one more than the other. Have a look at each column and see which you think most applies to you. Remember there are no 'right' or 'wrong' answers.

Extraversion	Introversion
I am motivated by new people, variety and change	I prefer individual relationships and stability
I don't like being out of touch with friends and activity	I need time alone – the outside world can intrude on my thoughts
I often act first, and think later	I consider before acting

Which best describes you?
- Extravert (**E**)
- Introvert (**I**)

2. HOW DO YOU TAKE IN INFORMATION?

Some people seem to rely most on *sensing* – that is, using their eyes, ears and noses to make sense of what is going on in the here and now. *Intuitives* prefer to interpret and understand what is going on around them and see it as part of a bigger pattern. They often speculate on what might happen in the future, based on what they have already learnt.

Sensing

I automatically find practical common-sense solutions

I dislike guessing and prefer hard facts

My mind is focused on the present

I have instant recall of details of past events

Intuitive

I prefer to use my imagination to try to do things differently

I'm happy to guess or come up with theories

My mind is on what might happen in the future

I am better at remembering patterns and connections

Which best describes you?
- Sensing (**S**)
- INtuitive (**N**)

3. HOW DO YOU LIKE TO MAKE DECISIONS?

Do you tend to judge things in a logical, detached way, deducing the answer using the *thinking* side of your brain? Alternatively, do you rely more on *feeling* – making your decisions more subjectively, taking account of your personal values and the impact of your decision on others?

Thinking

I concentrate on work tasks and goals

I can solve problems objectively and dispassionately

I accept conflict as part of relationships

Feeling

I give priority to the needs of others

I try to get everyone to agree wherever possible

I don't like rows and disharmony

Which best describes you?
- Thinking (**T**)
- Feeling (**F**)

4. HOW DO YOU LIKE TO LIVE YOUR DAILY LIFE?

Do you like your day to be organized and structured? *Judging types* like to be prepared – they plan projects and work through them until they are finished. *Perceiving* people are more casual, preferring to take things more flexibly as they come.

Judging

I work logically in planned stages

I avoid stress by anticipating deadlines

I set targets and routines

Perceiving

I start immediately and plan as I go along

I work best under pressure and close to deadlines

I resist any commitments that interfere with flexibility

Which best describes you?

- Judging (**J**)
- Perceiving (**P**)

What you should end up with is a four-letter code that you think best describes yourself.

From this test, I would describe myself as

■ The 16 personality types

Remember this not an exact science, and no particular combination is right or wrong. But to keep you thinking, overleaf are some typical features of each personality type. See how well you feel the description against your letter combination applies to you. After each description, you will also find a selection of jobs and career fields to which people in this group are often attracted. Don't worry if you don't fancy any of the jobs and employment fields in the list that follows your letter combination – it's only there to give you some ideas.

ISTP

Introvert, Sensor, Thinker, Perceiver

ISTPs tend to be logical, independent, objective and flexible. They are cool onlookers who can act quickly to find workable solutions when problems arise. They like the challenge of sifting through large amounts of information. ISTPs work in a wide variety of fields, including the public services and engineering. They usually make good technicians and mechanics.

Famous ISTP: Clint Eastwood

Jobs and career fields popular with ISTPs:
    emergency phone operator
    police and detection
    software developer
    information services
    medical technician
    commercial artist
    fire services
    sports therapy
    pharmacist
    animal trainer
    pilot, aircrew

ISTJ

Introvert, Sensor, Thinker, Judger

ISTJs are precise, quiet, realistic, honest and careful. They decide what needs to be done and work towards their goals without being put off. They are dependable and don't always like change. They tend to keep their feelings to themselves unless asked – at which point, however, they tend not to mince their words.

Famous ISTJ: C.S. Lewis

Jobs and career fields popular with ISTJs:
    business management
    accountancy

dentistry

teaching

meteorology

estate agency

construction

building inspection

information officer

credit analysis

doctor

medical researcher

ESTP

Extravert, Sensor, Thinker, Perceiver

ESTPs tend to be practical, adventurous, talkative and fun-loving. They prefer to act energetically to solve problems, and are bored by long explanations. They are friendly and well liked.

ESTPs have a natural desire to beat the competition, and can be highly successful at selling.

Famous ESTP: Jack Nicholson

Jobs and career fields popular with ESTPs:

retailing

stockbroking

prison officer

insurance agent

civil engineer

entrepreneur

marine biologist

police and private investigation

travel representative

professional athlete/coach

contracting and outdoor work

electronic games developer

property developer

ESTJ

Extravert, Sensor, Thinker, Judger

ESTJs ensure things get done – they are usually energetic, outspoken, friendly and productive. They are efficient organizers and like to create order. They often have traditional views and are opinionated and honest. ESTJs enjoy getting together with like-minded people and feeling they belong in the group.

Famous ESTJ: Margaret Thatcher

Jobs and career fields popular with ESTJs:
- business and management
- military and police
- information and press officer
- sports salesperson
- estate agent
- finance analyst
- health care administration
- database manager
- lawyer
- pharmacist
- insurance agent
- teacher
- property manager

ISFJ

Introvert, Sensor, Feeler, Judger

ISFJs are dependable, conscientious, organized and decisive. They are cautious and gentle, and work tirelessly for others. They prefer a stable, predictable environment. They do like to feel they are needed, and sometimes find it hard to delegate in case others don't do the job properly.

Famous ISFJ: Mother Theresa of Calcutta

Jobs and career fields popular with ISFJs:
- primary school assistant
- librarian and archivist

interior decorator

doctor, nurse, health worker

legal worker

customer service

counselling

office administrator

dietician

special-needs teaching

pub management

genealogist

ISFP

Introvert, Sensor, Feeler, Perceiver

ISFP types are friendly, down to earth, kind, thoughtful and faithful. They have a quiet sense of humour and might prefer to follow rather than lead. They tend to be modest about their own abilities, avoid arguments and like to work in their own time in their own space. They are often attracted to jobs involving serving others.

Famous ISFP: Paul McCartney

Jobs and career fields popular with ISFPs:

doctor, nurse

occupational therapist

designer

holistic and other therapist

customer service

fashion industry

chef

legal worker

surveyor

dental hygienist

travel agent, tour operator

medical assistant

alcohol and drug counsellor

ESFP

Extravert, Sensor, Feeler, Perceiver

ESFPs tend to be playful, curious, talkative and even impulsive. They are good company and love to meet new people and go to new places. They are also good at helping others adapt to new situations. They have common sense and are realistic. Occupations for this group are often service-related, but also include performance.

Famous ESFP: Elvis Presley

Jobs and career fields popular with ESFPs:
dental assistant
therapist
health worker
social worker
public relations specialist
radiology technician
occupational therapist
travel agent
tour operator
promoter
actor
performer
vet
events coordinator
marine biologist
store salesperson

ESFJ

Extravert, Sensor, Feeler, Judger

ESFJs like to put others at ease and tend to be friendly, talkative and always on the go. They are good at identifying problems, and they work and play energetically. They can get upset or wounded at times, but make natural hosts, paying attention to the smallest details to make people feel welcome.

Famous ESFJ: Julia Roberts

Jobs and career fields popular with ESFJs:
   estate agent
   personal trainer and therapist
   vet
   special education teacher
   shop owner, buyer
   personnel and welfare
   nurse
   home health worker
   athletic coach
   hotel manager
   travel agent

INFJ

Introvert, Intuitive, Feeler, Judger

INFJs are usually reserved and polite – independent, thoughtful people who bring an individual flair to their work, usually with a clear personal vision of what is best. They are productive and original and seek meaning in ideas and relationships. They like to champion people who need help, but choose their friends carefully.

   Famous INFJ: Oprah Winfrey

Jobs and career fields popular with INFJs:
   alcohol and drugs adviser
   health practitioner
   speech and language specialist
   researcher
   lawyer
   website editor
   writer and artist
   mediator and conflict-resolution specialist
   charity worker
   specialized teacher
   architect

INFP

Introvert, Intuitive, Feeler, Perceiver

INFPs are quiet, kind and sensitive. They are curious, original and quick to see possibilities and the good in others. They take a lot on but usually get it done – putting a personal stamp on all they do. Doing good deeds gives them quiet satisfaction.

Famous INFP: Lisa Kudrow

Jobs and career fields popular with INFPs:

therapist

researcher

editor

writer

translator

interpreter

lawyer and mediator

business trainer

actor

entertainer

university professor

social worker

librarian

fashion designer

website editor

art director

ENFP

Extravert, Intuitive, Feeler, Perceiver

ENFPs are outward-looking, friendly and talkative, and have the ability to inspire others. Their enthusiasm can be infectious and they never tire of coming up with new ways of doing things. They sometimes benefit from encouragement, but are adaptable, with good people skills, which they often use to help others.

Famous ENFP: Robin Williams

Jobs and career fields popular with ENFPs:
  management consultant and trainer
  educational software developer
  actor
  performer, entertainer
  journalist
  graphics designer
  advertising and art direction
  housing director
  psychologist
  inventor
  IT trainer and consultant
  child welfare worker

ENFJ

Extravert, Intuitive, Feeler, Judger

ENFJs tend to be friendly, sensible and organized. They are decisive and form strong opinions. They are great persuaders, communicate well and are tuned in to other people's needs and emotions. They are productive and love to help others. ENFJs are attracted to careers in the caring professions.

  Famous ENFJ: Martin Luther King

Jobs and career fields popular with ENFJs:
  advertising account executive
  therapist and holistic practitioner
  counsellor
  business trainer
  foreign-language teacher
  humanities lecturer
  fundraiser
  TV producer
  marketing executive
  writer, journalist
  social worker

INTJ

Introvert, Intuitive, Thinker, Judger

INTJs often like to work on their own, working up plans and coming up with theories and then testing them in real life. They are organized and have good long-range vision. They are self-confident, with a tireless ability to keep improving things, but without letting their imagination override their reliability. INTJs also have a smattering of disregard for authority.

Famous INTJ: Jane Austen

Jobs and career fields popular with INTJs:
    lawyer
    design engineer
    medical researcher
    IT network developer
    software developer
    psychiatrist
    cardiologist
    writer
    inventor
    media planner
    finance specialist
    business specialist
    webmaster
    architect

INTP

Introvert, Intuitive, Thinker, Perceiver

INTPs are quiet non-conformists who are open to new ideas. They are interested in understanding things through exploring and analysing how the world works. They are analytical, thoughtful, detached and easy-going, though they are not usually party animals.

Jobs veer towards the creative, the mathematical and working in the built environment.

Famous INTP: Albert Einstein

Jobs and career fields popular with INTPs:

photographer
internet entrepreneur/designer
architecture and design
business strategist
manager
writer and artist
editor
entertainer
lawyer
surveyor
computer programmer

ENTP

Extravert, Intuitive, Thinker, Perceiver

ENTPs bring enthusiasm and imagination to new projects and are generally friendly, outgoing, humorous and unpredictable. They like change and dislike routine. They enjoy debating issues and are good at reading others – a skill they often employ in their choice of jobs.

Famous ENTP: Oscar Wilde

Jobs and career fields popular with ENTPs:

marketing executive
design engineer
writer
artist
entrepreneur
banker and venture capitalist
business consultant
advertising director, copywriter
radio/TV presenter
political manager
property developer
actor

ENTJ

Extravert, Intuitive, Thinker, Judger

ENTJs are logical and friendly but strong-willed and often outspoken. They make demands on themselves and others, and are natural leaders with long-range vision. They like debate and discussion, and enjoy adding to their store of knowledge.

Famous ENTJ: Bill Gates

Jobs and career fields popular with ENTJs:

management consultant
politician
activist
business owner
lawyer
financial adviser
property developer
marketing executive
economic analyst
chemical engineer
educational consultant
doctor
computer specialist

■ It takes all sorts to make a workplace

Of course, no personality test, however extensive, is an end in itself. It's only a way of looking at yourself.

We all have dominant styles of behaviour, but nobody is entirely consistent. We should certainly not be slaves to our 'natural' personality traits if they sometimes get in our way or stop us from doing things.

For example, people who are good at maths are good at solving problems and usually extremely logical. If that isn't you, you might think a job involving problem-solving should be avoided at all costs. Yet you can use what you have learnt to work on and conquer your weaknesses. Just because maths isn't your best subject, it doesn't mean you can't assess a situation at work and come up with a practical solution.

So, don't say: 'I can't solve that problem or go for that kind of job because I'm not logical.' Instead, say: 'I may be a natural "feeler", but I can still look calmly at the facts and come to a logical decision.'

Learning about your personality type should also help you see why some things come easily to you, while others take a great deal more effort. When you get a job, it's likely you will encounter a mixed bag of personality types in any one office or workplace. It's then you will see that while this diversity is usually a good thing, it can also be the cause of rows and communication breakdowns. Sometimes it's easier to deal with people once you realize the way they respond to you is influenced by how they look at the world. Change the way you approach them, and things might run a lot more smoothly.

If you fancy trying some other personality quizzes, details of where you can find more online are on pages 221.

▓ Time to get organized

Changing your personality might not be possible or, more to the point, desirable. But there is one thing you can brush up on that really will help as you choose options and think about your career. So brace yourself – it's time to get organized.

Sorry to nag, but you're not going to get far if you can't keep track of the information and ideas you'll be working on. Nothing to do with how you are going to pay your way in life will be sorted out overnight – unless you win the lottery. And even that's no good if you've lost the ticket.

You might already be one of those people who has everything organized and in the right place – so you can lay your hands on names, places and phone numbers at a moment's notice. It's a habit worth getting into – not the pursuit of super-tidiness, just a little personal order, which will save you lots of time in the end. Like it or not, organization is a vital skill for life.

To find out where you stand on the organizational front, it's time to face the test. Answer the questions overleaf and then add up your score in order to find out how organized you are. Be honest – no point deluding yourself!

QUIZ: HOW ORGANIZED ARE YOU?

1. It's the weekend and you've got loads of coursework to do. Do you:
   a Write a list of what you've got to do and tick each piece of work off as you finish it.
   b Discover you've left most of your textbooks you need at school/college.
   c Do it on Monday morning on the bus.

2. Imagine you're going out with some friends for a pizza and then to see a film. Do you:
   a Suggest that you split the pizza bill equally, regardless of what everyone ate.
   b Remember to take the vouchers you have so you get a discount on the pizza.
   c Leave the money side of things to someone else to worry about.

3. It's your friend's birthday and he/she has been given an electronic organizer as a present. Do you think:
   a That's the most boring present in the world.
   b Your diary is just as good.
   c You fancy getting one yourself.

4. You have got an hour left before a big date. Are you:
   a Playing it cool – you intend to arrive 'fashionably late' to show you're not over keen.
   b Still watching TV and haven't had a shower yet.
   c Twiddling your thumbs and feeling nervous, having arranged a lift into town.

5. Which of these things is someone most likely to say about you?
   a 'It's amazing you can ever find anything in your room.'
   b 'I know I can always rely on you.'
   c 'If you had a brain cell it would be lonely.'

6. You have a geography project to hand in next week. How do you feel about it?

    a What geography project?

    b No problems – just got something to print off the computer.

    c Have started the research, but it's a bit of a rush job.

7. It's a maths lesson and you need a compass and protractor in class.

    a You always have the right equipment in your pencil case.

    b Although you had a new maths set for Christmas you keep forgetting to bring it to school.

    c What's a protractor?

8. You are put in pairs to work on a project. Do you:

    a Forget about it and let your partner do the work.

    b Suggest when to meet up to work on the project together.

    c Email some ideas to your partner and then phone up to see what they think.

9. Each day you have different work and subjects to study at school or college. Do you:

    a Pack your bag the night before so you don't forget anything in the morning.

    b Get your stuff together when you get up.

    c Often find you've brought the wrong books.

10. You need ID to get into college. Do you:

    a Occasionally have to go home because you've forgotten yours.

    b Frequently scrabble in your pocket or handbag but usually find it.

    c Think not having your ID is for wimps and you've always got yours.

SCORING

To score your test, give yourself the number of points shown against each of your answers (see next page), then add up your total score.

Question	a	b	c
1	10	5	0
2	5	10	0
3	0	10	10
4	0	0	10
5	0	10	0
6	0	10	5
7	10	0	0
8	0	10	10
9	10	5	0
10	0	5	10

So how organized are you? Let's find out.

Score 0–40

Hmmm … you're so laid back you nearly fall over. You need to get more organized or else you will miss out on things – both at school or college and in your social life.

Score 41–70

Not bad. You're organized enough to get through your day smoothly, but you don't let it stop you from having fun. Sometimes you might need to do a bit more planning before you rush into things or allow others to make the running for you.

Score 71–100

Wow – your middle names are 'Personal Organizer'. Bet you don't even brush your teeth if it isn't on your list of things to do! But, seriously, you are able to cope calmly with all the things life throws at you without getting stressed. Maybe you could occasionally afford to chill out, relax and just let things happen.

Key points

- Try to understand more about your own personality and style – see what your friends think. (You can help them do the same for themselves.)
- Start thinking about how you approach tasks and the kind of work that gives you most satisfaction.
- People with similar personality traits often share career preferences. Understanding yourself better may help you discover the kind of jobs that will most interest and stimulate you.
- Ask yourself if you are sufficiently organized – and if not, try to do something about it. It's a lot harder when you have an employer looking over your shoulder.

'Know first who
you are; and then
adorn yourself
accordingly.'

Epictetus (AD 55–135)

Chapter 4
What do you want out of life?

In this chapter you will find:

❏ Why it's important to understand what motivates you

❏ How to start identifying your goals in life

❏ How your work can enable you to enjoy the lifestyle you want

Ask teenagers what they want out of a job and most of them will probably talk about 'enjoyment' and 'interest' – but what exactly does that mean? Enjoyment means different things to different people and only you know what really interests you. So let's start with a very simple question – but one that is more complicated to answer the more you think about it:

Just what do you hope to get out of your career?

Well, money obviously – at its most basic, work is what we do to earn enough money to live. Sooner or later, we all need to pay for our own food, housing, clothes, heating, entertainment and the rest. Somewhere next in our priorities might come job satisfaction, a great bunch of like-minded workmates, perhaps ... then there's the chance to socialize, travel or meet people, a desire to earn respect from colleagues, status or regular promotion, a stimulating, varied work environment, personal intellectual challenges ... the means to pursue hobbies or interests ... enough extra cash to support other family members ... the list could go on for ages.

What's interesting is that if you asked everybody you knew to make such a list, we could almost guarantee that no two lists would be the same. What's more, people soon find themselves thinking not so much about their ideal job but about the things it would enable them to achieve in life itself.

When it comes to work, we all have a personal set of priorities that will change over time. Working out what these might be is not easy when you are still at school or college, but it can be a real help in choosing a career.

■ What are you working for?

This chapter, then, is not so much about work, but what you will be working *for*. We are all motivated by different things and each of us values some things more than others. So if you are not exactly getting excited about career opportunities, it could well be that you have not yet identified the skills you most enjoy using, or the values and goals that are most important to you in life.

Your current priorities might revolve around relationships, social life or exam results. Most people like to think they are free-spirited, and you might hope that money and practical issues should never dictate your priorities. Yet history suggests most people's financial outlook will change over time. It wouldn't be much fun being stuck on a low income simply because you never thought you would need a career that delivered you progressively more cash as you grew older. For example, your life plan for the next ten years could look like this:

go to university
get job
travel abroad/holidays
buy car
buy house
find partner/get married
have children
care for family members/friends with disabilities
pursue sports/hobbies
develop other interests or skills (e.g. music, languages)
volunteer
earmark time for busy (and expensive) social life

■ What is important to you?

You may think the list above does not represent what you personally want. No problem – write one that does! Then, when you have your list, think about how the things on it might have an impact on your choice of job. For example, if travel is high on your priority list, you need to think about what that means – do you want to travel before you enter university or start work, or after? And for how long? A month? A year? If you are thinking of a long period of travel, ask yourself whether you'd like to try to arrange a job to come back to on your return, or whether you'd prefer to keep your options open.

Equally, if you wanted to buy a home early on in your career, this might mean you would have to look for work in certain parts of the country where housing was affordable – or even search for employers offering preferential mortgage rates to their staff.

And what about children? Having children may seem like something you won't even think about for years, but if you're smart you won't ignore the possibility when you're career planning. Traditionally it's been women who have given up work to look after children or taken responsibility for arranging childcare while they go out to work. Nowadays that's changing. More and more men are taking an active part in bringing up children, and surveys repeatedly highlight the desire of working men to spend more time with their kids. A recent study even claimed that nearly three-quarters of fathers under 30 would give up work to be with their children if they could afford it. Whether you believe that or not, the fathers in your generation are likely to demand far more time with their kids than their fathers did, so don't make the mistake of thinking that family-friendly hours are an issue only for women.

Another key consideration is flexible working – no longer something only for would-be parents to think about. You might want flexible hours for all sorts of reasons to do with your interests outside work. Fortunately, it's becoming more common for employers to offer staff the chance to work non-traditional hours or to work from home for part of each week. Some – usually the larger or public-sector employers – also have schemes where you can apply for leave for long periods of time (career breaks or sabbaticals) on an unpaid or reduced-salary basis. If you intend to 'work to live' rather than 'live to work' – by which we mean that your career will not entirely dominate the rest of your life – you need to start planning for that now.

Think about your list and ask yourself how important each item is for you – is it something you really want or just a nice idea? Re-order your list with the most crucial job requirements at the top and the least important at the bottom. What you've got is a very basic picture of how you want your life to be. Now you can build on it.

■ Get your priorities right

We've looked at what's important to you in your life generally, but what about when you are actually at work? What would your ideal job give you in return for your time and effort? Money might again be at the top of your list, and then you might put job security, flexible hours, respect in the community or even a fancy job title. Here's a list of some of the most common work-related motivators. It's worth adding some more of your own so you can begin to build up a profile of how you would ideally like your working life to be.

financial rewards
good working conditions
good relationships with colleagues
opportunity to work in a team
opportunity to work independently
interesting/enjoyable work
opportunity to travel
job security
recognition and praise
opportunities for promotion

....
....
....
....
....

If you still don't know what you want, try looking at this the other way round. What *don't* you want if you can possibly avoid it? How about:

a dead-end job
a big debt before you start work
an insecure job
a boring job
a repetitive job
a job involving long or variable hours
to work alone
to work in a team
a grotty work environment
to work locally
a job that takes you away from family and friends

Maybe that has spurred you on to look for jobs that avoid some of these features. By producing priority lists along these lines you can begin to pinpoint sectors worth exploring. For example, if recognition and praise are important to you, you would need to think carefully before you opted for a career in an environment known for being high competitive, such as the City or sales. That's not to say that you couldn't find a job in those sectors that would suit you, but you'd need to recognize that the rewards there are traditionally financial rather than verbal. In other words, you'd be more likely to get a big bonus for good work than a pat on the back from your boss.

And don't forget to look at *all* the aspects of each potential career. For example, joining the army is rightly described as offering good opportunities for travel and promotion. However, if a high quality working or living environment were important to you then it might not be your best move.

As a rule, you'll feel highly motivated at work if you feel that you're playing to your strengths: using your skills and being challenged but not beyond the point where you're capable of doing the job well. We all want to be interested in our work, but not everyone wants to end up as managing director. It's not just a question of whether or not you are ambitious, it's more about how big a part of your life you want work to take up – and what you would give up along the way to get where you wanted.

So think about the skills you have and how far you want to climb up your chosen career ladder.

■ Buying into a lifestyle

Given our 21st-century obsession with 'lifestyle', you may not be surprised to hear that research shows that a lot of young people are now basing career decisions not so much on the actual job itself as the lifestyle they think goes with it. This means they look at a career like, say, engineering, retailing or financial services, and decide whether it appeals to them on the basis of the sort of people they think would do a job like that; the sort of life they think those people would lead both at work and outside, and what the workplace would be like.

Being motivated by the idea of having a particular way of life is not necessarily the same thing as being motivated by money. The lifestyle you like the look of may not involve highly paid work. Its appeal may be more subtle. For example, certain charities, such as Médecins Sans Frontières, which sends medics into disaster areas, have acquired a glamorous reputation though the work they do is obviously very far from glamorous. And working as an unpaid 'runner' for, say, a TV production company is often seen as a better job than more highly paid alternatives for lifestyle and image reasons.

Different jobs do have particular lifestyles associated with them and, as we outlined in Chapter 3, like-minded people do tend to gather together. But don't be over-simplistic. Not all media jobs are fast-moving and exciting, and the furthest you will travel working for some airlines may be the local bus or railway station. A legal career could mean living like Ally McBeal but it could also mean working for your local council, lecturing at a local college or being the in-house adviser to a manufacturing company. Imagining yourself doing a glamorous job is no substitute for exploring what individual roles actually involve.

■ Show me the money!

At its most basic, work is what we do to earn enough money to live. But you could scrape together enough to survive on by begging on a street corner. How much money we hope to earn relates to our expectations – and that is linked to what we have been brought up with or told we will have as adults. So money – and the fun we can have with it – is an important motivator, but it's not the only one that matters; a lot of the things you will enjoy in your adult life will have nothing whatever to do with hard cash.

Even so, 'a good salary' always comes out at or near the top of studies into what motivates young people. Jobs in accountancy, banking, computing, management, business and the legal profession are all among the top choices of people looking for a comfortable income – especially boys and older students.

If earning loads of cash is high on the list of your priorities when it comes to choosing a career, you're almost certainly thinking of going to university. But how much money will your degree earn you when you finally get a job? Your salary will depend on a wide range of factors, from your qualifications and experience to the state of the economy, the sort of work you're hoping to do and the part of the country you'll be working in.

If you think that the more qualifications you get, the more you'll earn, think again. Now that almost half of young people get degrees, competition among graduates can be intense, and some choose to continue their studies to enhance their CVs. However, while more letters after your name might tip the job balance in your favour, employers don't usually offer applicants with MAs or PhDs much higher salaries than ordinary graduates. Postgraduate studies are more about expanding your knowledge than your bank balance.

Having a degree does not necessarily mean you will be able to find a better-paid job open only to graduates. To give you some indication of what some of the best graduates are currently earning, here are some charts put together by the Association of Graduate Recruiters. The Association represents over 600 companies. Between them, they are responsible for filling a high proportion of all the graduate-only vacancies available each year. A glance down the lists clearly shows how much starting salaries can vary according to the kind of work and the part of the country where the job is based.

Starting salaries paid in 2003 by employers	
More than £35,000	1%
£30,001–35,000	6%
£25,001–30,000	11%
£22,501–25,000	10%
£20,001–22,500	22%
£17,501–20,000	43%
£15,001–17,500	6%
£15,000 or less	1%

Median starting salaries by business function or career area	
Investment banking	£35,000
Consulting	£28,500
Solicitor/barrister	£28,000
Actuarial	£23,500
Marketing, IT *and* General management	£21,500
Sales, Financial management *and* Accountancy	£21,000
Electric/electronic engineering	£20,600
Other engineering	£20,500
Human resources *and* Mechanical engineering	£20,000
Civil engineering	£19,300
Logistics	£19,000
Science/R&D *and* Retail Management	£18,500
Purchasing	£17,000

The *AGR Graduate Recruitment Survey 2004*, produced by High Fliers Research Ltd

Over the page you will find starting salaries organized by UK region, also as supplied by the AGR's 2004 *Graduate Recruitment Survey*.

UK median starting salaries by region	
London	£24,000
South-east	£21,000
East Anglia	£19,300
South-west	£19,100
North-west	£19,000
The Midlands	£19,000
North-east	£18,500
Wales	£18,500
Yorkshire	£18,500
Scotland	£18,500
Northern Ireland	–

As you will have seen, the highest salaries were offered by investment banks and consulting or law firms. But salaries for the same job vary widely from one part of the UK to another. For example, the AGR calculated that in 2003 the national average starting salary for graduates was £20,300. However, on average, London graduates got £24,000, while those in the North-east, Yorkshire, Wales and Scotland earned £18,500. These are big differences, even taking the higher cost of city living into account. (Figures for Northern Ireland were not available.)

▓ Stability and long-term earning power

On the face of it, salaries in fields such as computing and finance are attractive – particularly compared to jobs in areas such as teaching or nursing. Studies have shown that young people often enter these fields because of the financial rewards on offer. But you do also need to think about job stability. Computing and finance are both notoriously cyclical sectors. In other words, they go through times when employers need a lot of staff, followed by periods when redundancies are common. Contract work is also the norm, particularly in computing, which means that while you might earn a good salary for a fixed period of time, you could find yourself with no work and no income at other times.

Parents often place a great deal of emphasis on the earning potential of particular jobs. And it's understandable, since they have many years' experience of managing their own finances – and probably know what it's like to run short of money.

Sooner or later you might need to make some strategic decisions. Do you go for the job with the biggest monthly pay cheque and perhaps put up with aspects of work that you don't especially like? Or do you make financial sacrifices now, such as continuing your education, or taking a lower-paid job in an organization that offers you better prospects in the longer term? Having a clear idea of your life goals should make such decisions easier.

▓ Your priorities will change

It can be annoying when parents tell you that you will see things differently when you are older. But it is a fact that your personal circumstances are likely to change over time. For example, if you get into a long relationship with someone or have children, you will probably need to earn more. However, if your partner also has a well-paid job, you might choose to work flexibly or to start working fewer hours yourself.

One of the best ways to make sure you continue to enjoy what you do throughout your working life is to revisit your list of priorities from time to time – to see if your current job is a good fit. A lot of people never get round to doing this, and then wonder why they don't want to go to work in the morning. The important thing here is to remember to chase your own goals – not someone else's. Just think what your life might be like if you did exactly what you thought was expected of you. Within a few years you would probably be unhappy and exhausted.

The sad thing is that a surprising number of people do exactly that. They go through life trying to meet the expectations of their parents, teachers or friends without ever working out what is truly important to them. Identifying personal priorities over the course of your life might seem a blindingly obvious thing to do – but it's not as easy as it looks.

The chances are that you'll probably have to compromise on some of your original work priorities when you take a job. You might, for example, have to work a long way from your family or work unsociable hours for two or three years in order to equip yourself for a more ideal job. Unfortunately, you can't have it all.

▦ Motivation: the key to excellence

Much of this chapter has been concerned with trying to shape your work so that it delivers the life you want. But we should not overlook the huge personal benefits of managing to pick a job that suits you down to the ground. If you can't wait to get up and go to work to find out what the day will bring, it means you are highly motivated by your job. You are using skills you enjoy using and taking every chance to extend yourself.

Simon Cowell, one of the judges on TV's *Pop Idol*, often says that you cannot be a winner unless you possess what he calls the 'X factor'. It's impossible to define star quality, but most of us know it when we see it in the working world. Let's say you turn up late for a flight and there's someone who calmly reassures you, sorts everything out and really stands out in their job. Think about a teacher who has made a difference to your life, or a skilled salesperson who convinced you to buy something from them when you had planned to buy it elsewhere.

People who make their mark at work are almost always those who really enjoy what they do. Their jobs are delivering them what they want out of life. All the while, they are developing their skills ands adding to their knowledge. In short, they have found their natural roles in life.

Key points

- If you find choosing potential careers difficult, it's probably because you have not yet identified the skills you most enjoy using, or the values and goals that are most important to you.

- Stop looking at potential jobs in isolation and consider instead your personal needs and lifestyle requirements over the next few years.

- Remember that your financial circumstances will change and you may not be able to achieve all your life goals if you do not have the skills with which to gain long-term earning power.

'If you don't want to work,
you have to work
to earn enough money
so you won't have to work.'

Ogden Nash

Chapter 5

What kind of organization do you want to work for?

In this chapter you will find:

❏ How potential employers come in a variety of shapes and sizes – from multinational companies to public services and small local businesses

❏ How each style of organization offers different kinds of day-to-day work experience

❏ How to build a picture of where you'd like to be working in ten years' time

Imagine you are off to work for the day. What sort of workplace do you think you might be most happy to spend your days in?

How about a large and thrusting company, where you live on your wits, your reflexes and selling ability? The better you perform, the more money you take home. But you are right – there's a catch. Would you be quite so happy if you realized that you would soon have to look for another job if you failed to make your monthly sales targets?

Perhaps you might prefer to help customers or clients choose goods or services, or to spend your time in a public-service organization where making a profit is not the objective.

The point here is that the size and business goals of the enterprise you work for could be of as much interest to you as the job you fancy doing. Too many people end up having to go to work in a place they don't especially like. Not for nothing has the modern office been described as hell with fluorescent lighting. So it's important to think about the kind of employer and the size and working style of the company you are most likely to feel comfortable in.

Some people love the buzz of being based at a large headquarters complex, where things are always changing, there are plenty of outside activities and they can gossip with people of their own age and interests. Others prefer to work as part of a close-knit team – if possible, near to where they live or socialize.

Then there are those who actively prefer their own company to being with other people all the time. You might not want to start your own business, but there are plenty of roles that involve frequent travelling, being out of doors, or even working on your own for long periods.

■ Jobs serving the public

Around one in five of all the jobs people do in Britain are in the public sector. We're talking here about a vast array of tasks, without which the country would grind to a halt. The sector embraces everyone from the governor of the Bank of England to teachers, doctors, nurses, the armed and emergency services, postmen and women, civil servants and local authority staff. The public sector is the dominant employer in health and education, while the private sector holds sway in production, construction, and in providing every kind of service.

Until recently, the proportion of the UK workforce employed in the public sector had been gradually shrinking. In 1981, almost a third of us worked in the public sector. By 2001, this was down to under 20 per cent. One of the reasons for this is that many tasks, such as catering, IT and administration, had been 'contracted out' – that is, the jobs were switched to private companies who have to compete for contracts to do the work.

What do people who work in the public sector do?

IN THE PUBLIC SECTOR

26.5% work in education

26.5% work in the NHS

14% work in other local government jobs

12% work in other central government jobs

7% work in HM Forces

5% work in nationalized industries

3% work in social services

3% work in the police

2% work in other public corporations

Less than 1% work in construction

Office for National Statistics

More recently, however, the government has been investing heavily in the public services – notably in the National Health Service and in education, the two areas that have seen the fastest growth (see the chart on the previous page). This investment began at the same time as a long slowdown in the world economy and substantial falls in the share prices of companies quoted on the London stock exchange. High-tech businesses and their suppliers were also at this point still suffering from big losses and a lack of customers after the earlier internet boom and bust. It's not unusual for governments to increase their spending in the public sector to try to counter weaknesses elsewhere in the job market or the wider economy.

One benefit of this trend has been that the public sector has started to look more attractive to school-leavers and graduates. It's also providing employment for some workers displaced by the upheavals in the private sector. For example, some of those who lost their shirts when the high-tech bubble burst are finding the teaching profession is now a more attractive job option.

In a MORI poll of a thousand typical graduates, 32 per cent said they wanted to work for public-service organizations. This figure was just a tiny bit ahead of the percentage who wanted to work for large companies (31 per cent), and the number who wanted to find work with small or medium-sized enterprises (27 per cent).

As well as increasing public-service employment, the government has also been trying to improve the quality of public services. One of the features of this has been an attempt to lure high-quality potential workers with incentives such as training bursaries and 'golden hellos'. These are small extra cash payments for suitable recruits. This shortage of skilled and motivated people in the public service could work to your advantage if you have the right qualifications and attitude. As to pay, average starting salaries are slightly lower than in the private sector. However, wages are rising slightly more quickly, and employment, in the main, is considered slightly more secure.

■ Work with an attitude

People who work in the public services do tend to share a particular attitude or philosophy – a desire to help make life better in their chosen field. They often say that *making a positive difference* is an important reason for doing the work they do. Firemen, nurses and the police, for example, do a job everyone recognizes is essential for the public good, but this belief in the importance of the public service is also shared by thousands of people who work for local authorities, and by civil servants who work behind the scenes to ensure that the laws or policies the government wants to introduce can actually be brought in and made to work.

Most public service careers are clearly defined – it's possible to plot where you might be in future years if you do well. The work is also relatively family-friendly, and flexible-working arrangements may be available, depending on the role.

So what's not so good about these kinds of jobs? Unsurprisingly, *bureaucracy and paperwork* came out tops in a study by the government's own Audit Commission. Some things never seem to change.

■ Small can be beautiful

The vast majority of firms in Britain are small businesses. Many really are small – 95 per cent employ between one and 49 people. Next come what are often termed small to medium-sized enterprises – or SMEs. There are around 27,000 of these, employing 50 to 249 people.

Small businesses are firms run by a few people who have to take on all the jobs required to keep the firm in profit. The enterprise will often be led personally by the founders or current owners, who will have a financial stake in the business and may work long hours to get everything done.

If you choose a smaller company, you could well find yourself working in a limited physical space with a relatively small group of people. It might be informal and friendly – but don't kid yourself it'll be a breeze. The work is likely to be just as high-pressured as with a large firm.

Unlike a larger firm, though, your interview for a job with a small firm might be quite casual. Small firms often don't have the resources to spend training managers in state-of-the-art interviewing techniques, so the onus is more likely to be on you to make a good impression by asking lots of questions, rather than just sitting there and letting the interviewer do all the work.

■ Life on the small-business front line

At a small company, you would probably soon be involved in almost everything the firm did. If the company was going places, you would not only build up great experience, but could be in pole position for promotions and pay rises. And something else worth bearing in mind is that increasing numbers of tiny technology and service companies have close relationships with much larger clients. During the course of your work, you would make contacts that could be invaluable when you start looking for a job move. If you are good at what you do, someone else might even approach you first.

But working for a tiny firm can have its drawbacks. Some small or family-owned companies are what are sometimes termed 'lifestyle businesses'. That is, they exist to provide a certain standard or style of living for their owners and their families and are not necessarily going places. What that could mean for you is that having got so far, you might have to take your experience elsewhere. You could gain some great experience, but might have to move on if you wanted promotion, a substantial pay rise, or to progress in your career. There are plenty of people working today in small companies who wish they had moved on when they were younger.

Among the more common types of small businesses that employ graduates are accountancy and law firms, high-technology companies and leisure companies. One development in recent years is that small and medium-sized employers have become more interested in recruiting graduates than they used to be. In the past, university-leavers were often seen as too expensive to employ. Small-business bosses used to complain that graduates lacked practical skills, didn't want to get their hands dirty and had unrealistic ambitions for rapid progression.

But enterprises are having to become more professional to survive – and that means they need more talent. Anyway, when you consider that nearly half of all 22-year-olds will soon have a degree of some kind, graduates are becoming harder to avoid.

So if you particularly rate variety, early responsibility and the chance to have your work noticed, a smaller firm is well worth considering. But, equally, don't forget there are disadvantages to being a big fish in a small pond. If you perform badly, there may be nowhere to hide.

WORKING FOR A SMALL COMPANY

PROS

Chance of rapid involvement in many aspects of the business

You are likely to be given responsibility

Greater input into company procedures and future plans

See your ideas put into practice

You may have more say in your career development

Working as part of a small, dedicated team

Working hours may be more flexible

Less bureaucracy

CONS

Career path may be unclear

There may not be formal training – it will tend to be on the job

Need to work long hours as required to meet deadlines

Starting salaries often lower than at larger firms

Fewer benefits (such as a car, pension, health-club membership)

■ Big is beautiful – for some

For some, Britain's largest and most successful companies remain the number-one choice – the household-name firms that are generally in the forefront of manufacturing and services. Many are mere divisions of even larger multi-national groups, which aim to take the cream of each year's applicants and tend to have the resources to pay slightly higher salaries. But they are also extremely demanding employers. They want plenty of bang for their bucks.

Day-to-day life in a large firm can be very different from that of a small one. By and large, big businesses employ people to carry out specific tasks and there is often little incentive to do things outside your responsibilities, which you or your department will not get paid for.

If it is a large firm you have your eye on, you might be surprised to discover that in 2002 there were only 7,000 large businesses in the whole of the country – that is, enterprises employing 250 people or more. Many of these are among the FTSE 100 companies whose ups and downs dominate the financial pages of the newspapers (which you should, of course, be scanning each day to find out what is going on).

Large businesses usually base themselves in busy places with plenty of professional and skilled workers living within easy reach.

If you want to build a large-company career – in the media, finance, pharmaceuticals, engineering, or many other fields – it's important to start finding out more about the companies you want to target. For one thing, you will need to discover how they tend to recruit – and when. This may be through links with particular universities and institutions or at specific job fairs. They might also trawl for suitable young people via careers specialists in your own area.

■ Life in a large firm

You could expect to go through numerous selection procedures before bagging a job with a big company. You might well never get to meet the senior management. You would work in one or more large departments under a manager or supervisor. An entire floor or building might be devoted to a single task – for example, providing customer service or processing insurance claims. But there would almost certainly be established routes by which you could learn new skills, take responsibility and progress through the organization over time.

Competition is usually fierce in large firms. Your ability to progress would depend not only on your actual achievements but also on getting the attention of the senior managers who are on the lookout for junior employees with the highest potential.

But remember that senior managers come and go – it's not always easy to tell whose radar screen you need to be on. A good idea with larger firms is to try and work out which areas of the business are regarded as 'core' – that is, those that are making money or are seen as promising areas for future growth. If you're in an area of the company with limited business prospects, your own promotion prospects may also be limited, however fantastic you are. Yes, business life is unfair sometimes.

The voluntary sector

There is also a fourth kind of organization that has recently become more prominent in the jobs market – Britain's voluntary or not-for-profit sector. This covers everything from welfare groups employing a single paid manager to housing associations, trade unions and national charities such as the NSPCC, Shelter, Oxfam or Amnesty. As things stand, there are over 180,000 registered charities in the UK.

This is a very big sector of the job market with over half a million paid employees – that is more workers than are employed in the City of London, in farming or in the car industry. One in 50 of all UK full-time employees now have paid jobs in the voluntary sector. They work alongside three million more part-time and unpaid staff.

Among other things, voluntary organizations are defined as independent of government and business; as bodies that do not distribute profits to shareholders, and as groups that provide benefits to others as well as their own members.

The voluntary sector remains a favourite choice for people leaving the armed services or wanting a career change. It certainly offers a bewildering array of roles and ways of working, with much to offer those transferring their skills from other fields. But strong efforts are being made to attract a new, younger generation of workers. The largest charities have jobs that are comparable with many found in the private sector – from accountants, marketing and public relations officers to social workers, campaigners, lawyers and scientific advisers.

This is a job sector where you do need to consider carefully the kind of organization you will be joining. The work may be paid but you will need to be in sympathy with the aims and objectives of the charity or welfare group you hope to join. One of the best ways of doing this is to have already built up volunteering experience – your past record should go a long way towards convincing potential employers of your commitment to this type of work. It may not be the sector to choose if top pay is your priority, however (though some jobs are highly paid).

Interestingly, surveys have repeatedly found that not-for-profit workers are generally happier and more fulfilled than those in other professions.

■ Working in manufacturing

Although we don't have room to describe all the individual sectors of the job market in this book, we do feel it's worth speaking up for modern manufacturing. It is often overlooked as a possible career avenue, even by young people who are fascinated by designing and making things.

Mention industry to most people and a picture immediately springs to mind of people toiling in huge grim smoke-belching factories, or metal-bashing on scruffy industrial estates. The reality is that the motor and general manufacturing industry has changed almost beyond recognition in the last decade. Closures and cutbacks have been painful. Yet, at the same time, whole new areas are opening up in manufacturing to meet the demand for better-designed, higher-quality products.

The fact is that around 14 per cent of the population still work in manufacturing – that's over three and a half million people. Even so, the continuing loss of jobs and the negative press coverage have left the entire sector with a largely undeserved image problem. Factory work is too often – and wrongly – seen as the employment option for those who can't find anything else.

A while ago, a story was being told in manufacturing circles about a class of schoolchildren who were taken to look around a newly modernized, state-of-the-art factory. Its managers and staff were very proud of it – so were not pleased when they overheard a teacher say to the class: 'So remember, if you don't do your homework, you could end up here!'

Such attitudes are not only out-of-date, but demonstrate that sometimes teachers need a bit of re-education themselves.

If you're the sort of person who admires well-designed, up-to-the-minute and innovative products – everything from clothes to furniture or electronic gadgets – then creating the products of tomorrow could be your thing. Yet, according to an industry body, the Manufacturing Foundation, only one young person in 25 even *considers* a career in manufacturing because they see it as 'hard work, dirty and boring'.

What's often overlooked is that the factories that have survived or opened up more recently are clean, exciting, high-tech operations with informal, cooperative working conditions entirely unrecognizable from those of just a few years ago. Such operations may require far fewer people, but those that are employed rapidly become highly skilled and become part of teams deeply involved in developing and improving the entire production process.

The sector is likely to continue to experience problems but modern manufacturing is central to the UK's future. Continual innovation is at the heart of recent success in such industries as pharmaceuticals and biotechnology, aerospace, automotive, electronics and chemicals. What's more, with fewer people choosing to study subjects such as engineering, maths and science, manufacturing could be looking at a severe skills shortage. If you are good at these subjects, the manufacturing world of tomorrow could be a fantastic opportunity for you.

Even better, 67 per cent of young people surveyed by the Manufacturing Foundation who had spent time in a modern factory said they enjoyed the experience. So it's worth finding out more about the variety of roles on offer – one could be be right up your street.

Detailed information about all the different industry sectors and what they offer can be found on the Connexions website (details on page 219), which provides a regularly updated profile of the latest trends and opportunities.

■ What's your ideal working environment?

Thinking about your ideal working surroundings could guide you towards possible careers – or at least steer you away from the kind of environments you know you wouldn't enjoy working in. So this could be a good time to reflect on the different organizations described in this chapter and imagine yourself and what you might be doing in ten years' time.

Here are some questions you might like to consider.

- ■ Are you based mainly in the UK, or do you travel or work abroad?
- ■ Are you usually in an office, on the road, based at home or do you spend most of your time outdoors?
- ■ Do you work for a large multinational company, a medium-sized firm, a small business, or are you self-employed? (For more on self-employment, see Chapter 10.)

- Can you see yourself working in the public sector, for a voluntary organization or charity, or only for a commercial firm?
- Are you doing shift work, normal office hours or working part or flexible hours?
- Do you work with a large group of people, an ever-changing group, a small team, or do you spend much of your time alone?
- What kind of people do you work with? (For example, are they like you, or do you have dealings with people of different ages or outlooks?)

Now, can you describe your ideal working environment?

....

....

....

....

....

....

....

....

....

....

....

....

....

Key points

- The size and business goals of the enterprise you work for could be of as much interest to you as the actual field you want to work in.

- Most people working in the public sector have a desire to improve people's lives in some way. Pay may be a little lower but jobs may be slightly more secure.

- Smaller firms are becoming more dynamic and can offer rapid promotion and hands-on experience.

- Large companies are still a top choice for those wanting to build a professional career with established paths to promotion.

- Manufacturing does not have a good image but offers some great opportunities.

- Thinking ahead and imagining your preferred working conditions and the roles you might like to carry out will greatly aid your career search.

'Choose a job you love, and you will never have to work a day in your life.'

Confucius

Chapter 6
Tracking down jobs that might suit you

In this chapter you will find:

❑ Strategies and exercises to help you pick out job sectors that might suit you

❑ How to use job information to widen your choice of possible career avenues

❑ How to turn detective and quiz your family, friends and neighbours about their line of work

❑ More about Connexions and other careers services and how to use them

S o, you have discovered you are an extravert, brimming with potential ideas and keen to get started in business. There again, perhaps you are down-to-earth, caring and longing to get on a plane to see the world. Alternatively, you may just be confused. If you are uncertain about how you're possibly going to earn your living, no worries – you are perfectly normal.

A life of jobs

Picking a career might seem daunting because many people feel they have to come up with a particular job. However, working life isn't like that any more. A life composed of different jobs is more likely to be what's in store for you now. Some people will be lucky enough to move seamlessly from one role to another. Others may need to build up a 'portfolio' of jobs to keep them busy (see Chapter 8 for more on work in the 21st century).

All this means that, for the vast majority of young people, it's not realistic to work towards one single employment goal to the exclusion of all other possibilities. Instead, you need to build up skills that will make you attractive to a new employer so that you are not left high and dry if you outgrow your old job or are made redundant.

Almost every job changes over time, and employers much prefer taking on people who can demonstrate a real interest in making their firm more successful and profitable. They want people to tackle a wide variety of tasks, with the flexibility and willingness to apply their skills and experience to entirely different roles as required. So it really does pay to think about broad areas rather than specific roles.

This certainly applies to career selection. For example, if you're initially set on becoming a fashion designer, you should do as much research as you can and consider the many other possibilities in the wider field of, say, product design and consultancy. Could you imagine yourself designing home textiles, or advising a client on new uniforms for their workforce?

Let's take another example. Suppose your best subjects were maths and science and you had been told that good jobs were available at a local engineering concern. A little more research could lead you to discover that modern engineering offers a vast array of opportunities at home and overseas. Once you had found out more about these, you would be able to judge whether what was on offer locally was your best bet.

See if you can single out:

- The business sector or general area you think you'd enjoy working in.
- Where you might like to work – near to home, in another town, overseas?
- The kind of co-workers you'd choose to work with – young crowd, small team, experienced professionals, on your own as much as possible?
- How your ideal job would enhance or at least complement your overall lifestyle plans.

▓ Which sector might suit you?

You might think that no one knows you better than you do yourself – but that's not always true. It's sometimes a lot easier to spot other people's unique qualities than it is to pin down your own. So here is an exercise you can do with a friend who is also starting to think about careers.

Sit down, each with a pad and pen, and start listing every single quality you think best describes the other person. Put down as many as you can think of. There are some suggestions below to get you going. When you have both finished writing, swap your lists over so you have the one written about you in front of you. Now it's your turn to add anything to the list you also think is true of you – things your friend didn't think of.

YOUR QUALITIES

willing	responsible	steady-handed
creative	friendly	conscientious
ethical	sensitive	nimble
fast	caring	sharp-eyed
intuitive	selfless	squeamish
determined	imaginative	unsentimental
forthright	understanding	agile

resourceful	careful	supportive
able	energetic	communicative
discreet	honest	helpful
trustworthy	hardworking	flexible
thorough	dedicated	easy-going
organized	insightful	strong
precise	assertive	perceptive

When you've each done that, look through the following list and note down any of the activities or things that currently interest you, or you think might interest you in the future.

Don't just rely on what's listed here – see if you or your friend can think of anything else to add.

YOUR INTERESTS AND SKILLS

architecture	wildlife	art
creative writing	countryside	astronomy
cars	gardens	sailing
collecting	theatre	walking
keeping records	driving	organizing events
entertaining	travel	performing
designing	film	specialist music
decorating	TV	entertainment
danger	cookery and food	languages
playing music	fashion	health
sport	current affairs	finance
fixing things	computers and IT	hair
using maths	camping/outdoor	beauty
music	building	history
carpentry	science	geography
selling	craft	sea
meeting new people	books	crime

So now you should have two lists each. Next have a look at the following categories, which represent various sectors or fields of business activity where people are employed.

JOB SECTORS

animals	hospitals and health	police and security
aerospace	services	retail
banking and finance	hotels and catering	sales
building	internet/IT/computers	social services
government – local and	law	transport
national	manufacturing	teaching
engineering	media	telecoms
food	nature	tourism and leisure

Working down your two lists of personal characteristics and interests, see if you can possibly imagine a match with these or any other job categories. For example, if you have 'caring' in your first list, you might imagine yourself working with the RSPCA, doing something with patients in hospital, managing a health centre, being a wildlife warden, working with children in a hostel, or perhaps specialist teaching. So you'd tick animals, hospitals, nature, social services and teaching. If, say, you have 'design' in your second list, then you might have ticked aerospace, engineering, internet, retail, media or manufacturing.

That should give you at least a few ideas to think about. Remember, each area or sector encompasses hundreds of different jobs, most of which most of us might never come across in a lifetime. No exercise or quiz can highlight exactly the 'right' industry or career path for any of us. But this kind of process might set you off on a fruitful line of research.

■ Turn your interests and skills into a career

Most people know of someone who has managed to turn a childhood hobby or talent into a full-time job – a garage owner who started fiddling with cars at the age of six, for example, or perhaps a local journalist who always scooped the English prize for creative fiction at school.

Some practical interests offer relatively obvious job potential – things like handling animals, doing people's hair or sorting out problems with computers. (See Chapter 10 if starting your own business appeals to you.) Anything you feel strongly about might offer scope for working up into some kind of a career plan.

Have a good think about your personal opinions and ideas. Again, ask your friends to help list them. For example, you might have particular views about the treatment of children, health, the environment, or the workings of government. If you do, then don't waste all that passion. Spend a little time investigating careers in areas where someone like you could actually make a difference – for example, in the law, social or welfare services, in conserving the environment or some aspect of government.

▓ It's all on file

Once you've short-listed some potential sectors to explore, it's time to get stuck into some more detailed career research. Here, you're in luck. Never before has there been so much useful and helpful information up for grabs.

Your parents may have had to make do with a few dog-eared leaflets from a careers teacher, and probably spent hours sending out stamped addressed envelopes to various organizations seeking information about jobs and the necessary qualifications or training. Today, thanks to the internet, there's a wealth of information about working in business, industry and the public services that you can browse online from home, school or college at the touch of a mouse.

Try to discover more about firms that operate in the industry, trade, profession or service you are interested in and what kinds of roles their people fulfil. Most organizations now have websites, and many of the larger ones publish up-to-date information about how they recruit and the kind of candidates they are looking for. Professional and industry bodies also publish loads of useful information you can print out or download. Almost all of them provide links you can follow to member companies or other representative bodies that may be able to help you.

But even if you love armchair surfing, you can't do everything on the internet – well, not yet anyway. Don't forget good old-fashioned paper directories such as *Yellow Pages* and *Thomson*. These still have the most comprehensive lists of firms of all sizes in your area – from acupuncture clinics to zinc metal producers.

Almost every firm has to recruit staff at some time – so why not go and talk to those that take your fancy, or see if you can find anyone who works for them? If you're looking for a Saturday or holiday job, try a local company involved in something that interests you. It could be a great place to get an inside view of working life. (See Chapter 7 for much more on work experience.)

◼ Read the newspaper backwards

It's also a great idea to start reading the back section of a daily newspaper – and we don't mean the sports pages (unless, of course, you're set on a career in sports journalism). The business pages may not strike you as especially exciting or be the first thing you turn to, but they can be a mine of potentially useful information. After a while, you may be surprised at what a good feel they can give you for what's going on in various industries.

Take, for example, the extraordinary rise and fall of the dot.com internet companies of a few years ago – or the more recent transfer of many call centre jobs from the UK to Asia.

Stories connected to these events were all faithfully documented in the business pages long before they reached wider national attention. So if you do make a point of spending even a few minutes reading the business pages, you will be surprisingly well placed to judge for yourself which firms and even which whole sectors are on the up, and which may be facing problems or shedding staff.

Equally, if you are interested in working in the public sector or one of the professions, newspapers such as *The Times, Daily Telegraph, Independent, Guardian* and *Financial Times* carry regular supplements and feature articles covering specialist areas. You can always pop into a library to check them out and find out which are the days of the week when you should make a point of buying particular papers.

■ Make the best of your careers service

A good starting point for the latest information on occupations and how to prepare for them is probably the careers library at your school or college. The range and quality of the resources you will find there varies across the country, but almost all in the English state sector are linked to your local Connexions service (see below), so they should have access to a fairly comprehensive range.

Careers guidance in England

For those of you who haven't come across it yet, Connexions is a national support service for the four million 13- to 19-year-olds in England. It was set up between 2000 and 2003 to cut the number of 16- to 18-year-olds not in education, employment or training. It tries to do that by providing a one-stop advice and information service to help teenagers in a wide range of areas, including careers, learning, money, health, housing and relationships.

Connexions is there to help you overcome personal difficulties that might prevent you making the best of the education and employment opportunities open to you – from guidance about universities to counselling for drug dependency. It's a wide-ranging service but, specifically in terms of careers, you might find it useful when you're making big decisions such as:

- Choosing exam subjects
- Deciding between school or college
- Selecting and applying for vocational training or higher education courses
- Getting information and advice about different jobs and careers

How does Connexions work?

Connexions brings together all the services and support provided by a wide range of government departments, agencies and voluntary organizations. These include health and youth services, drugs action teams, and so on.

Even though the service is managed by the government, it is provided at a local level by 47 Connexions Partnerships, each responsible for their own part of the country. Each local partnership employs personal advisers to assist you with anything that might be concerning you, and they can put you in touch with specialist help if need be. The personal advisers come from a range of backgrounds, for example, the careers service, youth work and the voluntary sector, and their skills and experience vary. According to the Department for Education and Skills, their job is to raise aspirations, encourage learning and provide opportunities for teenagers to achieve their potential as they prepare for adult and working life.

You can get in touch with the service in a number of different ways:

- Via the website: www.connexions-direct.com
- By visiting your local Connexions centre (you'll find the nearest one in the phone book)
- Via your school or college
- Via your local community centre

What can Connexions help with?
Connexions staff should have the resources to help you with a wide variety of personal and work-related decisions. These include:

- **Education** Choosing courses for school, college or university, plus information about qualifications, funding for study, gap years and studying abroad.
- **Free time** Advice on how to put your spare time to good use, including details of local groups, volunteering, sport and other personal development activities.
- **Health** Everything to do with keeping healthy, including diet, sexual health, drugs and alcohol.
- **Housing** Your rights, help with concerns about leaving home and where to go if you are homeless.
- **Law and citizenship** Information about the law, including your rights and responsibilities as a consumer as well as a citizen.
- **Money** Information to help you with budgeting your money, opening up a bank account, details about benefits and the financial aspects of going into work or training (such as tax and national insurance).

- **Relationships** Information on building and maintaining good relationships with friends, family and others.
- **Travel and transport** Details about local transport and how to get about, including learning to drive and how to apply for your driving test.
- **Work and training** Details of opportunities locally, nationally and abroad. It covers your rights, job hunting, CV writing and training routes.

Independent schools

The Connexions service or its equivalent in other parts of the United Kingdom is available to young people over the age of 13. However, unlike in state schools, Connexions advisers aren't usually available to pupils in independent schools. They have separate arrangements for student advice and guidance. But don't worry if you are at an independent school and want to tap into the Connexions service. There's no problem with you doing that – you can still visit or phone your local Connexions centre (you'll find them in the phone book), or use the web-based advice service: www.connexions-direct.com.

How helpful is the Connexions service?

Having a one-stop shop where you can go with questions about such a wide range of things has got to be a good idea. It can benefit you to discuss ideas or problems with someone outside the circle of your family, friends or teachers. Whether you go direct or through your school, you should be allocated a personal adviser to help you.

The government argues that the great advantage of personal advisers is that they can give you impartial advice. And that is a very important point. For example, if you're thinking of leaving school at 16 and you discuss the possibility with your teacher or head of year, can you be sure that the advice you get isn't coloured by the fact that schools get more funding for each student they hold on to after they've reached 16?

The Connexions advisers are independent and detached from your situation. So, in theory, they should be a valuable resource for you. Like teachers, however, the quality of personal advisers varies. Some will be excellent, others less so. If you do land a good one, we suggest you make the most of the help that's on offer – it's free and you are not under any obligation to follow any advice you are given. If you're not happy with the quality of service you receive, don't give up on Connexions, just ask to see a different personal adviser instead.

Connexions is quite new and standards clearly vary across the country. The first Ofsted inspections of the service began in 2002 and the first reports were published in the spring of 2003. So far the findings have been quite positive – with some notable exceptions. You can check out the Ofsted website to see if a report has been published on your local Connexions partnership. Most of the partnerships still seem to be finding their feet.

As you'd expect, opinions vary among teenagers and teaching staff about how useful Connexions has proved so far, and their views are not always in line with those of the Ofsted inspectors. The service is a bit of a 'postcode lottery' – meaning that the level and quality of help and advice varies around the country depending on where you live.

The time you are allocated with a personal adviser may also depend on which school or college you go to – because the level of service is set in a yearly agreement with the local Connexions provider. Some schools and personal advisers are more organized than others. Some schools ask pupils to arrange a timed appointment for a careers interview with a personal adviser; others book personal advisers to come into the school on particular days and wait for pupils to drop by and see them.

In some areas teachers report that because of a shortage of personal advisers, one-on-one careers interviews have had to give way to sessions where one or two advisers lead a careers discussion with a group of pupils instead.

The shortage of personal advisers is highlighted in a number of Ofsted reports and it's clear that in some parts of the country there aren't enough of them to meet the needs of all the schools and colleges in their area. Some careers coordinators also complain that not enough of the advisers have yet received specialized training to give careers advice.

The main lesson from all this is – if you are not getting the help you feel you need, then make sure you ask for it, because it is your right.

Careers guidance in Scotland and Wales

What if you don't live in England? Much of the on-line Connexions information will still be relevant and useful for you. Local careers guidance and information is available at schools, colleges and universities throughout the UK and you can also tap into government-run careers advice specifically tailored for Scotland and Wales at the following websites:

www.careers-scotland.org.uk

www.careerswales.com

Northern Ireland was due to launch its own careers website in 2004.

■ Start window-shopping for jobs

Before you choose GCSE or A level options, get hold of a recent copy of the Connexions booklet *Job File*, and browse the A to Z of Jobs on the Connexions website (www.connexions.gov.uk). As the Connexions *Job File* puts it, you wouldn't buy an outfit without seeing if it fitted you – and the same applies to employment shopping.

Lists like this can give you an up-to-date picture of what hundreds of jobs actually entail. Most usefully, they will tell you what qualifications you need to do them. This will help you choose your options.

Reading through lists like these can become addictive. You soon realize how little most of us know about how people get to do even the most familiar jobs. For example, did you know that if you wanted to become a pilot and failed to get yourself sponsored by an airline, your training could cost you a whopping £50,000?

If you fancy civil engineering, there are at least four recognized ways into the profession – ranging from gaining a four-year Masters degree to a vocational route requiring less exacting initial qualifications.

Perhaps you like working on cars, but think you won't be able to get work until you can drive. No problem – you would discover that you don't need a driving licence to become an apprentice motor mechanic.

Or perhaps you are thinking about becoming a pharmacist. *Job File* explains that entry is by a degree offered at 16 universities. You would need a minimum of five good GCSEs and three science A levels, including chemistry.

You would discover that although two-thirds of pharmacists work in shops, others have roles in hospital, industry, research and development. Most jobs require well-developed social skills and many pharmacists have to run their own businesses. You could also start exploring related careers you might not even have thought of – how about dentistry or biomedical science, for example?

It's always important to take your research beyond what you learn from one source. Competition for places in some fields is such that, in practice, you would need more than the minimum stated qualifications to stand a chance of beating other applicants.

Let's take another example. Say you've been thinking of a job in the rail transport industry. You would discover that there are plenty of roles that don't ask for formal qualifications, but that you would be expected to pass tests of your aptitude, health, fitness, eyesight, colour vision and hearing. You would also discover that most companies prefer train drivers to be over 21. A Modern Apprenticeship leading to NVQs (see page 186) might be a good way to get started – but you would need to check if any schemes were available in your area.

So don't rely on whatever leaflets happen to be in your college or school library. You need details and up-to-date facts to make informed choices.

▓ Visit your nearest careers library

Among other things, careers libraries should be able to help you find out:

- ▓ Details of university and vocational courses
- ▓ What different jobs are like
- ▓ What training and entry requirements you need and how to get them
- ▓ What employment trends locally mean for jobs in the future

Pick any potential job you are interested in and the library staff should be able to help you find out what the entry requirements are, what training you need and how to get it, what courses of study you need to follow now and in the future, and where such courses are available.

So, if you don't know already, *find out where the library is!*

Your careers teacher, form tutor or school office will be able to tell you where it is and how to get there.

That's all well and good for those who have an idea what they want to do – but what about people with only vague ideas, or no ideas at all? Actually, this is where most careers libraries come into their own. If you are still undecided, there really is no need to wander round the place like a lost sheep. The library should have activities and information coming out of its ears to help you find out more about yourself and what kind of work might suit you.

Don't be taken aback if you go in with a specific query, only to find the staff respond by asking you more questions. The whole point of these places is to encourage you to compare employment options for yourself, rather than steer you towards specific jobs. So don't be put off. For a start, all career libraries should have access to suitable tests and quizzes to help assess your skills and aptitudes before letting you loose on the leaflets and resources. Make sure they print out any results for you to take home.

Again, all this is about what you want to do with your life – not what others think you want to do. That's why it's important to use the library intelligently and not just follow up ideas other people think might suit you.

Sometimes you can even get stuck on an idea that comes out of the blue. For example, carpet-fitter often comes up as a good match for young people who fill in questionnaires and aren't planning to go to university. You can see why this may be so – it's a job which uses practical skills, where you meet people, allows you to be your own boss, have regular work, and so on. No offence to carpet-fitters everywhere – we all need them. But it would be a bit of a shame if you decided a few years later that it would have been much more fun to be a deep-sea diver for the oil industry, or that you could have earned far more money being a bailiff, using your tact and diplomacy to enforce court orders.

Most libraries are open some lunchtimes and after school, and it's worth picking a time when they are not too busy so you can get your hands on the more popular resources. You probably won't be able to take any of the reference books away, but most have leaflets and booklets you can keep or borrow for a while. Don't rush it. There will be lots of new information to consider, so find out a few things at a time and go back for more later.

▓ It's all about you

One of the commonest and most helpful computer programmes available through careers libraries is KUDOS. The idea is to help you uncover the things that you are good at (or not so good at) and the activities you prefer, and to see how you respond to a series of questions on factors likely to influence your career choice. Using this information, KUDOS identifies occupations that might interest you.

KUDOS, and programmes like it, can help cut down a dauntingly long list of possible jobs to a more manageable number. Other good IT resources include the Careers Information Database and Careerscape. In each case, you should take home any suggestions and talk about them with your parents, teachers and friends.

Ask the staff to order you booklets about the job areas that interest you. Knowing more about the likely length of training, the intensity of competition, typical hours of work and the likely location of a job can influence and inform your choice. You should aim to investigate every single occupation that arouses your interest.

Have a look at the end of the book for more information about sources.

Classified information

Yes, it's true, almost all careers information is classified ... But it's not a secret. All you have to do is get your head around the way the information is filed in your careers library or Connexions centre. Currently, most of the data and literature is filed using the CLCI (Careers Library Classification Index). This system organizes information into groups. Section A contains general careers information such as higher education, job seeking or student finance information. Sections B to Y contain the job information.

However, in some areas, Connexions centres are organizing their data alphabetically along with their many other services. The new system is called CRCI – which stands for Connexions Resource Centre Index. Here, the nitty-gritty on jobs that you're probably after is filed in a Work and Training section, sub-divided into 23 job families. Each job family represents a different work sector – such as Building and Construction, Engineering, and Health Care.

Spend a while looking down the list and noting the sectors that interest you. For example, if you were thinking about working with animals, you would look for the relevant section and find information on jobs and careers in veterinary science, animal health and welfare, agriculture, fishing, nature conservation and horticulture.

It's worth remembering that every single employment category offers jobs requiring different levels of vocational or academic study and training – with salaries to match. For instance, if you are keen on animals and think you want to become a vet, you would have to spend up to six years studying, passing exams and building up practical experience. However, if you decided that becoming a vet is not for you, there are numerous other ways of working with animals you could start to research. For example, you could enter the field almost immediately as an animal welfare assistant or vet surgery receptionist.

Every job you come across will have its good and bad points. Each will demand different minimum entry qualifications and skills, and require different levels of knowledge and expertise. Some will be more specialized than others, or offer greater or lesser levels of responsibility.

▓ Comparing jobs and what to look for

What you should aim to do is to research widely in each of the sectors you find appealing. Don't try to rush this process – it will be time well spent. Try to compare the merits of each. Think about:

- ▓ What the actual job would involve each day
- ▓ The kind of people who do the job – and the skills they use to do it
- ▓ The range of companies or organizations in this field
- ▓ The entry requirements and training you would need to get in, and to progress

Making a list of the job aspects you want to avoid can also be helpful. Think of the personality traits you explored earlier and try to factor those in to your thinking. For example, if you don't like pressure or the idea of working in a large group of people, then a job in a call centre dealing with customers is unlikely to be the perfect choice for you.

Bear your longer-term goals in mind, too. Does the career path you are exploring:

- Match your skills, interests and preferred subject choices?
- Allow you to use or continue studying the subjects you enjoy?
- Offer you the kind of work environment you would thrive in?
- Have the potential to deliver the income and lifestyle you would like?

It may be that you are convinced a particular sector is right for you, but you feel it's too soon to make a decision on the kind of job you are aiming for. Depending on the field, it's often possible to keep your options open by choosing more generalized training or education and branching out later.

For example, if you were keen on some kind of legal career, you couldn't go far wrong by choosing a good law degree course. Alternatively, a general engineering course could give you a foundation in science, maths and computing skills and the ability to interpret data and to work in a team to solve problems – plenty of scope to branch out there.

General management training or business study courses are also popular options. But such a broad approach may not always work to your advantage if you have no particular goal in mind. If you are thinking of university, you might find it helpful to have a look at the Prospects website to see where students who studied different subjects ended up. (Details on page 220.)

■ Talk to people who know

One of the best ways of getting a feel for what it's like at the workface is to talk to people who do the jobs you're interested in. Strangely enough, it's something most people don't get round to doing.

Employers are skilled at making jobs look pretty exciting on their websites, and in publicity or recruitment material. But you should approach any of these as you would a holiday brochure. It's not so much what they say as what they don't say. Try to find someone who has worked for the firm and ask them. You might get a more accurate impression of what it's really like. However, you should also be aware that some people's views might be a little prejudiced, especially if they no longer work for the company or organization.

When it comes to checking out occupations, you could do worse than start with your own family, friends and neighbours. You may have strong feelings for or against following in your parents' footsteps or joining the family business, if there is one. But unless you ask, you may never even find out what one or both of your parents or relations actually do all day at work. Why not see if you can go with them for a few days during the holidays? Or persuade them to take advantage of the 'Take Your Sons and Daughters to Work' days, which large numbers of firms now participate in.

Make a note of the name of everybody you know who's working and the sort of work they do. Then, the next time you see them, you can play interviewer and ask some key questions. You can think up your own, but here are a few:

- What are the best and worst aspects of your job?
- How did you get the job?
- What qualifications did you need?
- What training were you offered?
- How much competition is there to get promotion?
- How much variety is there?

Do pluck up courage and ask around – most people are flattered by such interest. You might get the chance to go along with them and see their working environment at first hand. This is also the time to start some serious networking. It's not just friends who can help you – but friends of friends.

If you want to find out more about networking now you might like to jump to Chapter 12.

Follow up your research and the conversations you have by trying to look around as many different kinds of workplace as you can. Such visits can be very revealing. Few jobs are exactly what they seem.

A large factory might at first appear a confusing and impersonal place, but today most production workers are grouped in small interdependent teams, which can be extremely supportive and friendly. You might think working from home is solitary, yet people who do that might frequently travel to visit clients or have the freedom to pop out at lunchtimes to see friends – they might have a livelier time of it than someone stuck in a smaller office with the same handful of co-workers.

■ Job fairs are full of ideas

Another good way of sizing up potential careers and employers is by going to job fairs or exhibitions. Although these tend to be aimed at slightly older students or graduates, it's well worth going along to one if you get the chance. Having paid fortunes for a stand, companies are usually keen to give you brochures describing what they do and the kind of people they are trying to attract. You'll probably also go home with a stash of free pens, key rings and mugs.

Don't pre-judge any of the organizations attending, and certainly don't just visit those employers you've heard of. If there is one organization you especially want to impress, it is not a good idea to head straight there. If you are not practised in approaching employers, your nerves may get the better of you. Better to make a few practice runs with others first.

Companies exhibiting at a job fair or event might even be looking to sign up bright people as future workers on the spot. When you are old enough, some may be able to take you on a holiday placement or an after-college 'internship', which you may wish to start planning for. (There are specialist internship fairs you can go to as well.)

Some young people (and their parents!) like the idea of forging early links with a potential employer, and it can take some of the anxiety out of further study for those who want to know where they might end up. If this approach interests you, it's worth checking things such as how many students on place-ments return to work for the company. How many hours a week would you be expected to volunteer for and when? What skills could you gain? Ask all the relevant questions you can think of. You need to find out about the employer as much as they need to find out about you.

Learn the habit of asking for a business card and carefully noting the name of the person you talk to at any stand; when applying you can mention your earlier conversation.

■ Some firms may offer sponsorship

Some companies make a point not only of exhibiting at events but also of maintaining regular links with local schools, colleges or Connexions centres. Such firms want to maintain a steady stream of suitably qualified young people. They are ready to invest now to secure their future labour force – the people they hope will want to join them after they have been to university or gone through further training. By sponsoring students, organizations can attract young people before they get other offers. Work-experience placements or time with the company between studies allows the company to see people in action and make good use of their energy and ideas.

In practice, sponsorship involves students forging a link with a potential future employer and pledging to work for them before, during or after their studies. In return you get some pay or an extra grant to help towards the cost of your studies. Generally, sponsorship seems to be most readily available where there is strong demand for suitably qualified recruits – in areas including engineering, IT, science and business. Many deals of this kind do not oblige you to work for the company at the end of your studies if you really don't think you will get on. It should be a mutual decision.

■ OK, so you've found your ideal job

Clearly, many people don't reach this stage before leaving school, or even university. But if you do know your own mind, that's great – you have plans, something to work towards. Try to remain as flexible as possible, and talk over your plans with parents, teachers or friends. A lot can happen with your studies or in your life generally in the next few years to change your mind.

If you do have a specific job in mind, there are some crucial considerations, namely:

- What are the GCSE, university and/or vocational standards required? Be crystal clear about what the minimum entry requirements are for the work that interests you.
- How do you get there from here? Work out what steps you need to take from now on. What subjects must you include as part of your

options? Will you need to study for a degree, join a training scheme, or train on the job?

■ What's your back-up plan if things don't work out? Are there alternative ways into your chosen field, and what else would interest you in a similar or even entirely different area if you had to change direction?

■ Career shopping lists

Do keep lists of your career ideas – however bizarre – so you can follow them up whenever you get the chance. Some of the things you put down might be unlikely, but listing your ideas and then thinking over the pros and cons is a tried and trusted way of sorting them out. After all, you don't have to show your list to anyone if you don't want to.

■ Draw up your own job specification

Another approach that can be useful is to think broadly about your present and future skills, learning and employment preferences, and add any conclusions you arrive at to your list.

MY SKILLS

■ Do you like the idea of drawing on professional skills it took you several years to learn, or do you prefer the idea of gaining your skills while being employed?

■ Do you enjoy using communication skills to work with people or get the job done?

■ Do you think you could rely on using negotiation or persuasion skills to succeed in your job or get on with your colleagues?

■ Do you like the idea of using technical or mechanical skills as part of your work?

■ Would you like to be involved in the internet or IT as an architect, programmer or user?

■ Is being able to give free rein to your creative skills important to you?

The skills I'd like to use at work:

....

....

MY LEVEL AT WORK

- How senior do you want to become within your organization?
- Does being responsible for the supervision or direction of others appeal to you?
- Do you see yourself as a middle manager or a director?
- Will you be content to reach a certain level of responsibility or always be striving for promotion?

My ideal level would be:

....

....

MY ROLE AT WORK

- Do you see yourself managing others or carrying out a specialist role?
- Do you play a supportive role, anticipating the needs of others on your team?
- Do you enjoy working to deadlines?
- Are you designing or creating new products or services?
- Can you find new customers and sell them products or services?
- Does your ideal role involve measuring, analysing or supplying information?
- Would you be happy to repeat tasks every day, week, month or quarter?
- Would you like to be involved in teaching, guiding or motivating others?
- Would you like to talk to people in large groups?
- Is your overriding concern to help others?

My ideal role would involve:

....

....

■ Key points

- ■ See if you can pick out broad employment sectors you might enjoy working in.
- ■ Use resources you find online, at school or in careers libraries to find out more about the range of jobs in each sector. What does the work involve day to day? If you find it appealing, what subjects would you need to study and what are the minimum entry requirements?
- ■ Talk to as many people who are in work as possible.
- ■ Visit as many different kinds of workplaces as you can.
- ■ Think realistically about your ideal role at work. What skills would you use and how high would you expect to climb?

'The dictionary is
the only place
where success
comes before work.'

Anonymous

Chapter 7
Try some real work

In this chapter you will find:

❑ How work experience will help you build all-important *key skills* that will form the basis of almost everything you do in the future

❑ Why employers are so keen on seeing successful work experience on your CV

❑ How to plan and get the most out of your school or college work experience

There's one sure way you can improve your chances of landing some great jobs in the future, and that is to try your hand at some real work as soon as you get the chance. Any experience of working life you can clock up now will give you skills for the future.

Tasks such as baby-sitting, looking after animals, working in a shop or office, or even just helping a friend or neighbour all demonstrate that you are responsible and trustworthy. Although you might not realize it, the people who offer you such jobs are your first 'employers', and they will almost certainly be glad to give you a reference that will help when you apply for other work.

▧ Real work can build up your confidence

Not everybody is able to find the time for paid casual employment. Today, school work and commitments have become so all-absorbing that you may feel you have no time even to consider taking an after-school or weekend job – or volunteering for something. In many ways, this is a pity. Now, more than ever before, employers expect to see early but tangible signs of your personal abilities, confidence and individuality. Good social or people skills are not just a desirable extra, they are a 'must' for almost any job you can name.

Real work brings you into contact with people of different ages and backgrounds that you would probably never meet in the normal course of your school or student life. If you are naturally shy, it's even more important to build up your confidence. You might find you meet others in the same boat.

▧ Brush up on key skills

You might think that earning some cash and meeting new friends are the biggest benefits of finding yourself a casual job. Yet even short spells spent working 'for real' are great for developing your key skills. These are the skills commonly needed for success in education, work and life in general.

Most employers will ask you about any work experience you have, and the benefits you think you have gained. So, what they are looking for? Well, key skills you really can't do without are:

- **Numeracy** Using arithmetic in practical situations.
- **Communication skills** Talking and writing appropriately for a particular audience.
- **Information technology** A working knowledge of computers and how to use them.
- **Flexibility** The ability to work both independently and cooperatively with others.
- **Problem-solving** Being able to assess problems and come up with solutions.
- **Evaluation** Being able to constantly improve your performance through learning.

Unless your heart is set on being a hermit, you'll almost certainly need all these skills to do a good job. The great thing is you can practise them in your early work experience. Look upon it as invaluable free training – at someone else's expense! (For more on what employers are looking for, see Chapter 9.) For example, if you worked in a shop or office you might use computer programs, graphs or tables to price or order goods. You may learn to communicate effectively with difficult or elderly customers, to solve problems that arise while you are on duty, or to work with other members of your team.

Keep a note of any particular projects or situations where you have developed skills so that you can add their details to your CV and send it to potential employers, or mention them during an interview. If you do find a job, take time out every so often to review your progress – you might be surprised to see how much experience you have gained. Consider:

- What skills have you learnt, or discovered you already have?
- Which skills have you particularly enjoyed using?
- Which key skills do you lack, or need to develop for the future?

This approach can be especially helpful if you have managed to find some work experience relating to a job you would like to do full time in the future. It could give you ideas about how much you would enjoy such a job and what training you might need to succeed in it.

■ What work are you allowed to do?

No one under the minimum school-leaving age is allowed to undertake any tasks that are likely to be harmful to safety or health, or do any work that will affect attendance at school. Only 'light' work is allowed.

If you are 13 years old In England and Wales, children of 13 may do certain jobs specified in local by-laws, which can be checked through your local council offices. For example, a paper round is usually acceptable.

If you are 14 or over You can work part time in places like shops and local businesses, or do things such as baby-sitting for relatives or neighbours. Certain jobs remain off-limits, notably working in commercial kitchens and theatres or collecting money from house to house. You can be paid to take part in sport, advertising, modelling, plays, films, television or other entertainment, but your employer must apply for a licence from the local authority.

If you are 16 but still at school Once you are 16, you will be able to undertake a wider range of strictly casual and part-time jobs, but there are many restrictions. Until you have left school, the law states that you cannot have paid employment:

- During school hours on any school day
- For more than two hours on any school day – or for more than 12 hours in any school week
- For more than two hours on a Sunday
- For more than eight hours (five hours if you are under the age of 15) on any day
- Before 7 a.m. or after 7 p.m.
- For more than 35 hours a week (25 if you are under the age of 15)
- For more than four hours without a break of one hour
- At any time if it stops you from having two consecutive weeks of annual holiday from school

No one under school-leaving age is allowed to be employed:

in a factory or in construction work

in transport

in a mine

And if you are determined to leave school and go to work …

Don't forget that you cannot get a full-time job unless you have left school first. If you are 16, you need to wait until the last Friday in June. And before you get too excited, the new minimum wage for 16- and 17-year-olds will be £3 per hour, so don't expect to make your fortune.

■ Saturday jobs are worth having

Unless you live in a remote area, you will probably find there are more part-time, casual work opportunities around than you might have imagined. You might start with car washing, looking after your neighbours' pets or gardens, or offer a baby-sitting service.

Once you are 16, places like shops, restaurants, supermarkets, amusement parks and hotels may be happy to employ you at weekends or during the holidays. Think about temping in a favourite shop or local supermarket. You might like to try your hand at being a waitress or waiter, or help with the running of an office. Consider tourist attractions in your area, or working for a farmer or grower. If you are sporty, there could be some temporary work going in a local fitness or health club.

It's always a good idea to think through what skills you can already offer and take it from there. You might want to approach companies direct where you see young people already working. You could also think about looking closer to home – if cleaning, pet- or plant-sitting isn't for you, perhaps you have computer skills. How about offering to teach people how to use a computer or the internet? Think about the talents you have and consider who might be glad to make use of them.

■ Voluntary work can lead to a career

If you can manage without the money, voluntary work of some sort can be especially valuable. Many schools and colleges operate long-established volunteer programmes. If yours doesn't do this, your local Volunteer Bureau, Youth Service, Citizens Advice Bureau or even just the town or village noticeboard would be a good place to start looking.

Employers are generally keen to recruit people who care and are committed to helping others, and will usually be impressed by candidates with a volunteer track record. Looking after elderly people or animals, getting involved in campaigning or handling money as part of a school or club activity can all open the door to potential careers as paid professionals. People in senior jobs in welfare, campaigning or financial organizations often say they owe their position to early volunteering experiences in a school or college sixth form.

■ Try your chosen sector for size

If you can find part-time or casual work in the job sector you're interested in, then you really do have a chance to see what goes on. Even a low-level job can give you a worm's-eye view of the realities of life in that kind of enterprise or organization. You'll be in a great position to have a sniff around and to pick the brains of 'insiders' doing the type of work you hope to do in the longer term. Most jobs have their pros and cons, and you can put yourself in a better position to judge if this is still the direction you want to go in.

How you get on might surprise you. Consider the experience of one student we know, who had always been keen on becoming a hospital doctor or paediatrician. She was able to spend an afternoon helping and observing on a busy ward. What she discovered was that although she believed she could cope with the academic demands of the training, she was uncomfortable making conversation with the patients. In short, she decided she was not cut out for the job, and is now happily studying law instead.

Unfortunately, because of the law and the requirement to provide insurance, many volunteer roles are only open to those over 18, but it is sometimes possible to find lighter duties or to help someone you know – and gain some valuable insights into the bargain.

■ Make the best of your work experience

In most parts of Britain, something strange happens for two weeks in May or June. A secret army of 15-year-olds pours into the offices, stores and service businesses of an entire local area. Welcome to Work Experience Fortnight.

It's tempting to see the whole exercise as a plot hatched by secondary-school teachers to get you out of school or college for a couple of weeks. In fact, Work Experience Fortnight is a huge organizational task for schools. But the schemes do seem to work well in most parts of the country, and offer many young people the only chance they get to sample the real world of work. So don't waste the opportunity.

If you can get a placement in a field you are already interested in, so much the better. But remember, your school is probably arranging several hundred placements at the same time, so it could be a question of pot-luck. Participating schools and colleges have a standing list of companies willing to take young people. However, most also allow young people to find their own placements. So if you discover that what's on offer is not up your street, it may be worth asking relations and friends if they have any useful contacts or ideas about places that might take you on for a couple of weeks.

Choosing your placement

Think about what you hope to get out of your work experience. For example, is it to find out more about an industry, to check your practical skills, to see if you like office life, to improve your confidence?

Look at the placements on display. Don't rush into a decision or be influenced by your mates. **Read** the job description. Where is the job exactly? What does the employer expect? What should you wear? What time are you expected to start and finish? Should you take your lunch? What breaks are there? Do you need to see the employer for an interview before the start day?

When offered a placement, be sure you are clear what you are expected to do and who you will report to. Also make sure they explain health and safety requirements to you.

While on your placement

- Give yourself plenty of time to get there. Being late would be a big mistake.
- Speak clearly and shake hands firmly when you meet new colleagues for the first time. Smile and make eye contact with people you meet.
- Always follow your employer's instructions when working.

- Dress appropriately. Don't even think of chewing gum or smoking.
- Have a word with your work supervisor if the placement is not as it was originally described.
- Keep busy and don't be idle. Ask for more work if necessary and make the most of it – they might ask you back and even pay you next time.
- Aim to become 'one of the team'. Don't be afraid to ask questions and involve yourself in workplace activities.
- Expect a visit from a teacher, who will check you are OK and the placement is going well.

When your work experience is over

Think about what you have learnt, good and bad, so you can write it up and speak about your achievements.

- Was the work you did the sort of thing you'd do if you worked for a similar company as a full-time staff member, or did your employer only use you to do odd jobs?
- Was it the work you liked or was it the people you worked with who made the job enjoyable?
- Was it that *particular* shop, firm or organization that you liked or disliked or would you feel the same way about *all* such places?
- If you didn't like your job, was the reason you hated it more to do with the fact that the place where you worked was a dump or a real pain to get to rather than the job itself?
- Did you get on well with your manager? And how much did that have to do with your feelings about the job?
- If you didn't like the work you did, were there different jobs in the same organization that did appeal to you?

The National Council for Work Experience (www.work-experience.org), which supports high-quality work experience, asked some young people how their placements might help them in the future. Here are some of their replies:

'It gave me a better idea of the realities involved in working a 9–5 job. It also made me realize that I didn't want to do that job in particular!'

'I have been offered a job at the same company.'

'I gained in confidence and maturity and developed my communication skills.'

'I am hoping to work in education and feel my experience of working with students on a one-to-one basis, from very different backgrounds than my own, was very eye-opening and taught me a great deal.'

'It has helped me to identify the things that I don't enjoy doing, and some things that I do enjoy too. It has equipped me with technical skills that may be useful in future jobs, and more general "soft" skills that are transferable.'

What those young people had to say about their work experience speaks for itself, so do all you can to make the best of yours. And if it didn't quite work out, do consider having another go off your own bat – with a bit of planning you might be able to find somewhere else to sample work for a week or so in the next school holidays.

Key points

- Work on those key skills – you won't get far without them.
- There's no better way of getting a feel for the world of work than having a go at doing some real work yourself – however basic the job.
- Volunteering or work experience and a good reference can make all the difference on your CV.
- Doing work for real can build your confidence. It can help you discover more about how you get on with people and what skills you already have or would like to develop.

'It's work, Jim,
but not as we
know it.'

Dr Spock, *Star Trek* (altered)

Chapter 8
Work in the 21st century

In this chapter you will find:

❏ How new technology is transforming Britain's workplaces

❏ Why many people have more than one job

❏ Why workers are under ever more pressure to be highly productive

❏ Which sectors are on the up, and why 'personal service' jobs are on the rise

Choosing your ideal job should be that much easier if you first spend a little time thinking about what work in general might be like over the years that you're going to be a part of it.

Not so long ago, there was a widespread belief that by this early part of the 21st century we would hardly need to go to work at all. Modern machines and technology would do most of it for us. We could all pop into an office for an hour or two, and then spend hours on end enjoying our favourite sports or leisure activities.

Although the leisure facilities we have now would have astounded our great-grandparents, and they certainly provide increasing employment, most of us never seem to have time to enjoy them. So if you want plenty of time to sit on the beach, you are going to have to come up with a job that's a pretty good earner to achieve your ambition.

If you want a great example of how work now dominates our lives, compare some of the latest adverts for Coca-Cola with those that appeared in its early days. In 1917, happy Coke drinkers were seen sunbathing, sitting on a swing or killing time at a café. What a contrast with a recent advertisement for Diet Coke. It read as follows: 'Seven Meetings. Seven Locations. Six Cabs. Fortunately, your evening is free.'

And yes, it's true – UK employees work longer hours than workers almost everywhere else in Europe. Only time will tell if Britain's adoption of the EU's Working-time Directive will start to reverse that trend. But it could be worse. North American workers get a lot less holiday – many are still allowed only two weeks off every year.

The sheer pace at which work is changing has accelerated in the past 20 years. Digital technology has a huge amount to do with it. But there are other reasons, too, such as changes in the way we choose to live and spend our money and leisure time. Twenty years ago, who would have thought that DIY would become an almost universal hobby, or that nail bars and continental coffee shops with wireless internet access would be on suburban high streets?

Such shifts in society are inevitably reflected in the sort of work that needs doing. New types of jobs are being created, while others become redundant as employers find they can complete the same tasks more efficiently with fewer people.

Needless to say, some young people now thinking about employment will spend their lives working in a similar way and perhaps even in a similar occupation to their parents. But others will break new ground by earning their living in ways not even imagined a few years ago. It's a fascinating and challenging time to enter the workforce, with exciting career opportunities opening up all the time. So before you reach any final decisions about the work you'd like to do, take a few minutes to think about the big picture.

New jobs for new times

Now here are some jobs for anyone determined to do something different. How do you like the sound of being a ubicomp technologist, or a bioinformatics specialist? Or perhaps you fancy your chances as a longevity consultant?

The job titles might sound crazy, but if City and Guilds, the vocational examination board, have it right, these could be among the professions of the near future – and could become as familiar as shopkeepers and accountants are today. (If you want to know what those strange-sounding jobs involve, see the end of this chapter for a deeper insight into the work you might be doing – and the jobs that could be on the wane.)

New technology and changing lifestyles are transforming the British job market. In our lifetimes – in fact, within the next decade – dozens of careers will fade away or be forced to change. Fortunately, some new ones will take their place. For example, postmen and women and milkmen may find themselves in decline – but it could be boom time for personal dieticians, psychologists and plastic surgeons.

The big picture

Two hundred years ago, the advent of the steam engine started a revolution as industry and invention overtook land and farming as the source of national wealth. Just as the railway age brought disruptive change, so the internet and new technology are profoundly changing our working lives all over again.

It's hard to believe, but the World Wide Web was invented little more than a decade ago. Yet it is already one of the many new forces that are changing the way everyone works. We can't predict what the working world will look like for future generations, but we can say that the successful enterprises of the future will be those with the most skilled, creative, innovative and enthusiastic workers.

As politicians never tire of telling us, 'enterprise' is the lifeblood of our economy. What they mean is that our future success depends on people like you starting and growing new businesses that will provide a source of employment, competition and new ideas. Larger firms, too, will need people who can spot opportunities, take the initiative and adapt their areas of work to changing circumstances. Inevitably, some organizations will streak ahead and others will fall by the wayside.

It is this kind of change, or 'churn' as it's sometimes called, which results in people having to change jobs more often – jobs are more mobile than ever before.

Across the UK, around 26 million people work for their living. The majority are based in offices, shops, hospitals, schools and colleges – or spend part of their time on the road moving between one workplace and another. At the moment, there are still around three million more men at work than there are women. But that's changing. By 2011, it's estimated that a million more women will have joined the workforce.

■ Goodbye manufacturing, hello services

The most obvious change in Britain has been the long-term decline in manufacturing. Forty years ago, almost half the working population had jobs directly associated with making things. By 1995, it was down to less than one in five – and the number is still falling. Ever since, as factories have closed or been automated, most of the replacement work has involved providing services of one kind or another. It is widely forecast that almost two million extra jobs will be created in service industries. In particular, transport, distribution, hotels and catering are likely to recruit more workers. (This doesn't mean that manufacturing is no longer a sector to consider – see Chapter 5.)

A growth area will be personal services. Rising incomes, fewer people living in traditional family units and most of us simply living longer will all create demand for new services to keep us well fed, looking good and feeling physically and mentally fit.

For example, we'll need more hairdressers, and we'll visit ever larger numbers of therapists of all kinds. As Roger Bootle of Capital Economics recently put it, in the economy of the future there will be ever more pedicures, leg waxing, face cleansing and personal training.

New personal services such as 'time consultants' are forecast to spring up. These are individuals who get paid to organize busy people's homes, gardens and social arrangements. It has even been predicted that 'fun workers' will be employed alongside the rest of us with the sole idea of finding ways to make work more enjoyable and productive – kind of 21st-century court jesters.

This is all good news for those with practical skills. Call-centre jobs may be vanishing overseas, but at least there's no risk of all these pampering jobs being exported.

For those keen to spend longer studying for the jobs of the future, science looks a good bet. Take ubicomp technology, which we mentioned earlier. That's the means by which everyday objects can communicate with each other. You might, for example, be designing a fridge that can sense when milk is running low and order a delivery.

City and Guilds predict that 'longevity consultants' will emerge, with the sole job of helping retired people make best use of their later years. Dating agencies are likely to flourish – matchmakers may scour the world to find clients the perfect date. Fortunately, some things won't change – pilots are forecast to continue to fly high, as are tax advisers and tutors. Insurance brokers and estate agents are expected to have much less job security.

◼ Regional differences

Many of the manufacturing jobs lost during the 1980s and 1990s were in the north of England – as were most of the coalmines, which were closed around the same time. A whole generation of workers found it tough trying to cope with the loss of their traditional employment. Many were unwilling or unable to retrain or move to where jobs were available.

TRENDS IN UK EMPLOYMENT BY SECTOR – PERCENTAGE CHANGE PER YEAR

Sector	1990–2000 (actual)	2000–2010 (forecast)
Agriculture	▼ 2.9	▼ 1.2
Mining, electricity, gas, etc.	▼ 11.6	▼ 3.9
Manufacturing	▼ 3.3	▼ 2.6
Construction	▼ 3.4	▼ 0.4
Distribution & catering	▲ 0.6	▲ 0.9
Transport & communications	▲ 0.3	▲ 0.5
Financial & business services	▲ 3.2	▲ 3.3
Public administration & defence	▼ 0.3	▼ 1.0
Education & health	▲ 1.4	▲ 1.9
Other services	▲ 3.3	▲ 2.8

Wilson 2001

Now British workers are getting a little better at adapting when employment circumstances change. Today's job-seekers are measurably more adventurous, more flexible and prepared to travel longer distances to find the work they want. This is just as well, because regional differences are likely to remain for the foreseeable future. Your local Connexions centre, for one, should be clued up about your region and so able to help you make an informed choice about whether your best job prospects might lie further afield.

If you are worried that you might end up without a job, there's good news. Recent history suggests your chances of remaining unemployed are reducing. In 2001, less than 5 per cent of the working population were without a job – that compares to 11 per cent in 1986.

■ Welcome to part-time Britain

Looking back, the 20th century may come to be regarded as the century of the full-time, permanent job. By contrast, the 21st century may prove to be the century of part-time and self-employment. Already almost a quarter of the entire UK workforce is part time. A high proportion of such jobs are concentrated in catering, care and office work – far fewer are in areas like construction and manufacturing.

Companies are employing growing armies of part-time, temporary or seasonal staff. They rely on bringing in workers to do specific tasks on special contracts. Firms are also increasingly reliant on self-employed consultants – part of the army of so-called 'knowledge workers', many of whom may once have had full-time posts with the same organizations.

In the future, employers will continue to take every opportunity to reduce their costs by switching their supply of labour on or off at will. This means that some people may be asked to go part time, or will not be replaced by a permanent worker if they leave. All this could affect you directly – some of the work you might be interested in doing may stop being conveniently packaged in the form of a 'proper' job.

■ One person, several jobs

Increasing numbers of people will have a 'portfolio' of two, three or even four jobs, which they do during the course of the week. Some might do this out of choice – others out of financial necessity.

If one employer cannot offer sufficient work to fill a week, or the whole of a year, it makes perfect sense to look for additional jobs elsewhere. This is nothing new in itself – seasonal jobs have always been a feature of seaside resorts and agriculture, for example.

What it does mean is that if you want to get experience with a 'flexible' firm you might have to work hard to get noticed. Systematic on-the-job training and apprenticeships might not be available. You will have to use your initiative to find out for yourself what opportunities are out there – and keep more than one opening in mind at the same time. It could also mean that if you have your eye on a particular field you might have to swallow your pride and offer to work for nothing, or act as a low-paid 'runner' or 'gofer' to get yourself started.

Not so long ago, the cyberpope himself, the founder of Microsoft, Bill Gates, made a guest appearance on the US TV show *Frasier*. Makes you think when even the boss of Microsoft seems to be assembling a portfolio career.

■ Why workers have to deliver

Like it or not, almost as soon as you get your first job you will be judged against others on how productive you are. For example, how much business do you bring in, how many customers do you deal with, or how many problems can you solve for your employer in a day?

One of the main reasons for this is globalization: the technological revolution in our lifetime that enables information and goods to travel much faster than ever before. Customers can often scour the world to find the cheapest deal for the goods or services they want to buy. Companies that don't run efficiently will find that the prices they have to charge to make a sale are too low to cover all their costs and produce a profit. This is why businesses need to strive hard to make unique products they can charge more for.

Another important development is that companies almost everywhere in the world have access to the same computer technology and to all the latest management thinking to help them become efficient. This leaves the cost of workers as the only variable – the only costs that can be cut if times get tough. This is obviously a big issue in countries like the UK, where staff cost up to six times more than they do in, say, Bangalore in South India. It goes some way to explaining why call-centre jobs are being exported there.

It's also why employers have become so focused on extracting the maximum value out of their people every minute they are at work. Whole layers of unproductive middle management have been stripped out of companies. Organizations that used to employ large numbers of secretaries and clerical assistants now have few or none at all.

Increasingly, the old divisions between the people who make the decisions and the people who carry out the actual work are fast disappearing. Being able to type and handle a computer is no longer a skill in itself – it's a basic requirement. You made the sale – you also have to prepare and send out the necessary paperwork. Whether you end up being employed or self-employed, you will need to master a range of technical and administrative skills. For example, can you see yourself managing things such as budgeting, planning, purchasing, scheduling or quality control?

The stark truth is that those who are unwilling to add to their skills risk finding themselves having to compete for a dwindling number of less well-paid jobs – so called Macjobs, named after a certain chain of well-known hamburger restaurants.

■ Wherever I lay my laptop, that's my home

A few years ago, it was predicted that up to half the workforce would soon be giving up commuting and operating from home instead. The trend is gathering pace – but not quite as quickly as many predicted. About a million people in the UK are now home or tele-workers – proportionately far fewer than the numbers working at home in Scandinavia, Eastern Europe and Germany.

Working from home can be lonely, and you do need to be self-disciplined. It's important to have a clear dividing line between home and the area which is the 'office'– even if only to have somewhere that work materials can remain undisturbed. Some people say they have to physically walk out of their front door and come back in to go to work. Others, lucky enough to like what they do, enjoy blurring the lines between 'work' and 'the rest of life'. They also need self-discipline – but sometimes it's the self-discipline to stop work and pay attention to family members. Generally, this is more likely to be an option taken by people who are already established in their field. There may never be a complete substitute for having a good gossip with your work-mates round the water cooler.

The buzz words today are **flexible working** – that is, using the latest in digital wireless technology to do your job at home, on the road or at your company as your work tasks or appointments dictate. This kind of existence can give you a little more personal control of your own working life – and some time at home when you really need it.

In Britain, BT is among the organizations to have experimented the most so far with this style of working – 70,000 of its staff now work flexibly. But firms are not doing this out of the goodness of their hearts. Not having to house so many staff in offices is saving BT £180 million a year.

■ Ten cold jobs

Courtesy of City and Guilds, here are some of the jobs forecast to decline in the UK between now and 2010.

POSTAL WORKER The number of postal workers is expected to fall. For a start, moves to stem huge economic losses by the Post Office will result in job cuts. At the same time, increasing use of online and digital communication is expected to reduce the demand for letters. Postal occupations will also evolve and require different skills – for example, a shift from simply delivering items to specialized courier services requiring the use of IT for parcel monitoring.

PRINTER PC-based desktop printing and publishing is becoming so sophisticated and relatively cheap that fewer jobs need to be sent out to printers. A quick comparison of the quality and cost of ink jet and laser printers now compared with ten years ago gives some idea of the rate of developments in this area.

INSURANCE BROKER Larger numbers of people are expected to buy their insurance online. This is not to say that people won't need professional advice, but even this will be available via the web. Those brokers that remain will need to offer specialized services for customers who want the personal touch.

CLERICAL WORKER Many basic clerical functions are gradually being replaced by information technology. You might have expected this to happen much earlier – computers have been in many offices for 20 years. Until recently, however, companies had not fully integrated their various IT systems and still generated vast quantities of paperwork, often dealt with in large 'back offices'. The emphasis is now on productivity, and paper-based systems are at last disappearing in both small and large organizations.

MILK DELIVERY Ever more people are buying milk from the shops or having it delivered as part of larger orders from online grocers. Entire families go to work early before the milk can be delivered. All this is reducing the viability of local milk rounds. Some people might want to maintain milk deliveries to their homes, but the small numbers of such households will probably ensure it is no longer economic to run milk franchises.

ESTATE AGENT Almost all agents now use the internet to display the latest available properties and also to provide an easily accessible service. Customers can view information and print out details about any place near or far. Online delivery is reducing agents' costs, and over time this is forecast to reduce charges and to reduce the number of people employed in estate agency offices. Some agents may switch to charging fees for services such as house valuation.

CAR DEALER Some local dealers are expected to close as large companies and car manufacturers increase their grip on the market, selling vehicles online or from large, convenient and heavily advertised 'supersites' in strategic locations. Such operations enjoy economies of scale when compared to smaller dealerships, so can sell cars for less.

NEWSPAPER BOY/GIRL Within a decade, all national newspapers are likely to provide the option of receiving the full text of the morning newspaper online. This does not mean that newspapers will no longer be printed and bought, but there may be sufficient online consumption to make early morning delivery services uneconomic.

FARM WORKER Farming in the UK has weathered many storms in recent years, but incomes remain low and many more agricultural workers are forecast to seek other jobs, such as working in tourism. Future reforms to the EU's Common Agricultural Policy may lead to some subsidies to farmers being replaced by income support, giving people fewer incentives to keep working the land.

TELEPHONE OPERATOR Developments in voice automation and the increasing use of overseas call centres will lead to dramatic reductions in the number of people in the UK answering or handling telephone inquiries. Larger firms may further dispense with switchboards and operators.

■ Ten hot jobs

So much for the jobs going cold. Which jobs are hotting up between now and 2010? Here are some possibilities:

PLASTIC SURGEON All the signs are that cosmetic surgery will continue to boom. We are living longer and there is a marked desire in the western world to remain 'youthful'. There is also a growing celebrity culture – what was once deemed the sole province of the famous is now seen as widely acceptable. Long-term growth in real incomes has also provided people with the means to pay for surgery, and technological advances have opened up an increasing array of treatments.

GOLF PROFESSIONAL Thanks to the popularity of top players like Tiger Woods, golf has become 'cool' and is attracting younger people of both sexes from a broader range of social backgrounds. More players means more lessons and equipment, thereby increasing the demand for golf professionals. Much larger numbers of people are also now buying custom-made rather than off-the-shelf equipment.

TAX ADVISER The UK tax system is becoming ever more complex – even tax advisers admit they get confused at times. As incomes rise and the number of top-rate taxpayers increases, more people will find they have to pay one kind of tax or another and will have to seek specialist advice. A range of tax-based incentives has also been brought in for entrepreneurs and small firms – but business usually needs help to make the best of them.

AIRLINE PILOT The demand for air travel has always run faster than general economic growth, and the trend is likely to stay on the up as low-cost airlines continue to provide ever more flying opportunities to everyone from retired people with time to travel to gap-year students visiting far-flung places for work experience. More air travel means a greater demand for planes and pilots. However, technological developments could make pilotless planes possible within the next 20 years (whether passengers like it or not).

AIRCREW Whether it is a digital autopilot or a real live one in the cockpit, all these new planes of the future will require crewing, servicing and other essential services to keep them flying in and out of the UK.

TRAVEL CONSULTANT The growth in the number of travel consultants is largely down to the same factors identified for pilots and aircrew. However, demand for specialized travel consultants is also growing, and reflects increasing individualist attitudes. Consultants focus on specific market segments and establish niche operations. For example, there are consultants who are experts in five-star small luxury hotels around the world, and others who specialize in American golf holidays. These niche operators satisfy the increasing demand from people who know what they want but don't have the time to find it.

PSYCHOLOGIST Increasing numbers of psychology graduates will be looking for work, and fortunately for them it is predicted that the demand for psychologists will grow over the coming decade. Professional counsellors will play a role in helping people deal with personal difficulties such as divorce and family breakdown, which are on the rise. There is also likely to be a growing interest in 'life coaches' as individuals seek outside help to try to understand their own abilities and needs, and what they should do next in their careers. Some of this help may be provided by employers for their staff.

COMPUTER SECURITY CONSULTANT Commercial organizations already invest considerable amounts of money in securing their IT systems. The more dependent we all become on computer networks linked with the internet, the more even the smallest enterprises will want to take all possible means to ensure their data is safe from attack. This means huge potential growth for computer security specialists and consultants.

PRIVATE TUTOR Rising parental concerns about the quality of their children's education will lead increasing numbers of parents to spend money topping up their children's education by employing private tutors. Should more evidence emerge of universities discriminating against applicants from private schools, some parents who would have chosen private education might decide to put their children in state schools instead, but make sure they get plenty of extra tutoring.

HOME-CARE NURSE People are living longer, yet the cost of full-time residential care is likely to remain prohibitively expensive for large numbers of individuals. One solution may be the employment of more nurses who can provide paid care for people in their own homes.

▓ Ten hottest jobs of the future

OK, now we're getting into the realms of speculation. But here are some of the crazy and not-so-crazy jobs some of us might find ourselves doing from 2010 onwards.

NANOTECHNOLOGIST Billions are already being spent every year on nanotechnology research. The essence of nanotechnology is the building of unimaginably tiny structures – atom by atom – for incorporation in our bodies, the environment and almost any physical object we deal with. Profitable developments in nanotechnology could be seen within the next five years. There could be new drugs, fuels, lubricants, textiles, sensors, computer hard drives, memory and optical components – the list goes on and the potential for new roles is considerable.

UBICOMP TECHNOLOGIST Ubicomp could be one of the next big things in technology. The word is a combination of 'ubiquitous' and 'computer'. The idea is that large numbers of people will be involved in working out how to cheaply embed everyday objects with microprocessors, tiny sensors and transceivers. If they succeed, anything from furniture to a food container could sense changes in its state and transmit this information to the user. Your cupboards would know when stocks of provisions were low and order more – perhaps your book would sense when you were on the final chapter and order the next volume from Amazon via your computer. It's been described as the opposite of virtual reality. Instead of putting people inside a computer-generated world, ubiquitous computing will force the computer to live in the world with people. You could be part of an army of ubicomp technologists that emerge over the next decade to help make it happen.

BIOINFORMATICS SPECIALIST Since the completion of the Human Genome Project in 2001, the new understanding of the human DNA sequence has opened up a vast area of research under the general heading of bioinformatics. Biology and chemistry are merging into a new field offering enormous potential to tackle tumours and disease – but one requiring the next generation of information technology to process and compare vast amounts of complex genetic information.

FUEL CELL TECHNOLOGIST We've already invented cars with a fantastic environmental benefit – all that comes out of their exhausts is water. These vehicles run on hydrogen fuel cells, and President Bush has committed tens of billions of dollars of US government funding for research in this area. Fuel cells generate electricity from hydrogen. One of the snags is that the fuel is very expensive and there's much still to do in developing better ways to produce and distribute it.

TIME CONSULTANT As people juggle work and family commitments, there may be increasing demand for time consultants to help households and businesses better manage their time. Home services might include finding hotels and booking holidays, organizing gardeners and cleaners, food shopping, and supervising plumbers, builders and electricians. At work people may benefit from the services of special time auditors who can help them run their businesses better.

LONGEVITY CONSULTANT Longevity consultants will provide professional advice to an ageing population, helping them to stay healthy, look after their finances and enjoy a wide range of leisure pursuits. The average age of the population is expected to increase from 38 in 2001 to 45 in 2040. For the first time, we are entering an era when people can expect to spend two decades in retirement prior to death. Tomorrow's 'groovy greys' will want to do all they can to make the most of their time and money.

PERSONAL DIETICIAN AND TRAINER Celebrities and the well-off have personal trainers today, but in the future, and in an age of rising affluence, many more people will see the benefits of getting professional help in taking the right exercise and eating the right diet, Significant growth in demand is seen for dieticians, trainers and lifestyle gurus.

FUN EMPLOYEE In 2002, easyJet advertised in the national press for a new position as Head of Fun. While people naturally smile at such an idea, the underlying logic is that employers should strive to make work enjoyable, so that staff turnover falls and the firm becomes more productive. Many jobs have repetitive or unpleasant aspects, and the idea is that 'fun workers' will be given free rein to discover ways of improving routine tasks.

GLOBAL MATCHMAKER Matchmaking or 'dating' services have been around for a long time, but there could be a trend to establish them on a global basis. This has the obvious potential benefit of widening the catchment area should a client be looking for a particular type of mate. In an era of increasing globalization in business and travel, cross-cultural barriers to international relationships are already declining and will decline further.

WEBUCATION ARCHITECT Management gurus have already speculated that online education could become the greatest economic opportunity of the 21st century. Internet learning is still in its infancy, and given the global demand for knowledge, online delivery of lectures, coursework and tutorials could reap huge cost savings – set against the fixed costs of a college or university campus. The secret to success will be the design of course material, and it is here that the role of the webucation architects will be so important. Webucation architects will be teachers and lecturers with the ability to communicate and inspire learning online.

■ Key points

- ■ Within the next decade, dozens of jobs will die or be forced to change, but exciting new ones will take their place. If you are interested in a particular industry or job, it's worth considering where it might be in a few years' time.
- ■ The 21st century could prove to be the century of part-time and self-employment. Paying staff is an employer's greatest expense, and the work you want might not always be packaged in the form of a traditional single job.
- ■ In some fields, you may need to assemble a portfolio of work to keep you going.
- ■ There are fewer career ladders to climb where you can count on others spotting your potential. You will need to take responsibility for your own career moves.

EMPLOYER: boss, dead loss, superior, chief, commander, leader, high-up, bigwig, manager, supervisor, overseer, foreman, gaffer, head honcho, big cheese, top dog, big kahuna.

(Dictionary definitions)

Chapter 9
What do employers want?

In this chapter you will find:

❏ Why you have to sell your skills

❏ What employers want from you

❏ How to behave at work to maximize your chances of doing well

Much of this book is about what you hope to get out of a job. In this chapter we're going to turn the tables and look at what employers might want from you in exchange for your salary.

Almost wherever you want to work, you probably won't impress a potential employer unless you can convince him or her that you have the necessary communication skills and are a good team-worker. To progress, you will need to get on with colleagues of all ages and backgrounds. You have already probably heard mention of the so-called 'soft' or people skills – even the need to possess what is called 'emotional intelligence'.

These may be among the skills employers are looking for, but they do not come naturally to everyone. For example, you might be brilliant at maths or finance, but to get promotion in a bank you would have to learn how to keep your clients happy, manage priorities, cut costs, be assertive and take the lead in finding new ways to make money. There's an old joke that defines a finance clerk as someone who is good at numbers but never had the personality to be an accountant. The reality is that whatever the job, you'll need the personality.

And before you start to tackle all that, there is an even trickier task awaiting you. You have to convince that employer you are the right person for the job.

◼ Learn to sell yourself

When you finish your education and go out looking for a job, your role in society changes forever. All the time you're at school or college or university, teachers and lecturers are paid to teach and guide you, while your role is to listen and learn. They are the 'suppliers'; you are the 'consumer'.

When you go looking for work all that changes. Suddenly you're not the consumer any more – you're selling. The consumer is the person you're trying to persuade to employ you – your potential boss, or at least the person who's interviewing you on behalf of your potential boss. To get the job, you have to sell your skills, your experience (such as it is) and your potential. That transformation takes place overnight but it involves a major attitude shift on your part. There are still a lot of people out there you can turn to for help – careers advisers, parents, siblings, friends – but selling yourself to employers, who may or may not want to become consumers of your skills, will be something you need to become good at.

Even if you reach the top of the tree you still have to keep selling – chief executives may be in charge of their staff but they still have to answer to their investors or shareholders. Self-employment is not so very different either – there you'll find yourself selling to customers or clients as well as your financial backers. Even charity workers have to sell the aims of their organizations to people in the hope of a donation or help.

Employers want to invest in staff who are willing to learn the job, who want to progress and who will benefit the company, skills that are not always taught at colleges and universities. But what do they want in practical terms? Well, top of the list comes flexibility.

■ Flexibility

If there's one word that sums up what employers want from their staff nowadays it is 'flexibility'.

In the past, it was the skills employees had – skills that were directly related to their work and to managing other people – that were most likely to give companies a competitive edge. Now, ideas have changed, and flexibility is seen as the key to competitive success. In practice, this means you should never be a slave to routine or procedures, but always look for ways to do your work more effectively and efficiently. In large companies particularly, this involves being able to listen, communicate well and influence others to see things your way.

So what do employers mean when they say they need 'flexible workers'? In broad terms they mean:

- ■ Staff who are open to new ideas
- ■ Staff who are prepared to continue learning new skills throughout their working lives
- ■ Staff who accept new ways of working
- ■ Staff who adapt quickly to changes at work
- ■ Staff prepared to move house or go abroad for their work if need be

Many employers now want to be able to require their staff to work irregular or long hours as necessary, and they only want them on the payroll as and when they need them. So they recruit workers on short-term contracts or as freelances. Doing that works well for employers because they don't have to pay redundancy if the time comes when particular staff are no longer needed, and they can also save money on employee benefits like pensions, sick pay and holiday pay.

Having said that, flexible working conditions can work brilliantly for staff as well as bosses, because they can make it possible for you to balance your work with all the other things you want or need to do. The trick is to make sure that the arrangement your employer wants works for you too before you sign on the dotted line.

■ Absenteeism

When it comes to staff what most employers really want is a hassle-free existence: i.e. employees who get on with their jobs – and the other staff – without causing any problems, such as repeatedly turning up late or taking a lot of time off work.

Absenteeism is an expensive headache for bosses and it's on the rise. Obviously people need to take time off when they're sick, but recent research estimated that a third of workers aged between 16 and 24 take a day off sick each month when there's nothing wrong with them – so-called 'duvet days'. And most of them say they would stay at home with only minor ailments like colds or hangovers. If you want an easy tip for impressing your future boss, try turning up for work on a regular basis.

■ Staying put or moving on

Recruiting and training staff costs serious money and bosses are also looking for people who are likely to stay with them for a reasonable period of time so that they don't have to go to the expense of re-recruiting and re-training a new person a few months down the line.

So how long is a 'reasonable period of time'?

People tend to move from job to job more frequently at the start of their working life than they do later on, and it's not unusual for first jobs to last only about a year. Employers know that most first-jobbers will move on sooner or later but, having said that, it won't do your CV any good if you change job too often even in the early stages of your career.

You might feel wary of getting stuck with one employer for too long at the start of your working life. When the Association of Graduate Recruiters asked students in 2002 how long they expected to stay in their first jobs, most of them reckoned they'd move on after one or two years; only 2 per cent of them expected to be with the same employer five years down the line (see chart). In reality, most of them will have seriously underestimated their stay-time. In the same year, employers reported that 94 per cent of the graduates they recruited 12 months earlier were still with them, as were 79 per cent of graduates taken on three years previously, and 61 per cent of graduates who'd started work with them five years before.

HOW LONG DO YOU ENVISAGE STAYING IN THE FIRST ORGANIZATION YOU WORK FOR?

Up to 6 months – 3%	5 years to 7 years – 2%
6 months to 1 year – 13%	7 years to 10 years – 1%
1 year to 2 years – 28%	10 years to 20 years – 1%
2 years to 3 years – 18%	More than 20 years – 1%
3 years to 5 years – 10%	Don't know – 22%

Gradfacts 2002 published by the *Guardian* in partnership with the Association of Graduate Recruiters (AGR)

Working for the same organization for a number of years might sound boring but the chances are that you won't be doing the same job for the whole time. As you gain skills and experience you're far more likely to work through a series of different – and increasingly testing – jobs that will present you with a range of challenges. If that's not the case, then it's probably time to find another job.

According to the Chartered Institute for Personnel and Development (CIPD), an employer who plans to invest a lot of money in your initial training will expect you to stay in the job for at least two years. Later in your career you'll probably average between two and five years per job, but statistics like this need to be treated with caution because the norm varies widely across the various employment sectors. (If you want to get an idea of average stay-times in particular sectors, the relevant professional and trade bodies can help you.)

How long you stay in a job is something you'll need to think about throughout your whole career. In contrast to your grandparents' day, when employers were generally happy to see staff stay on the payroll for many years if not their entire working lives, now people who don't move on are often perceived as unmotivated or even lazy. Younger bosses, in particular, can often feel uncomfortable about managing people older than themselves, and workers who've been dutifully doing the same job for years are particularly vulnerable to being labelled 'dead wood' and shunted to the top of the 'prime candidates for redundancy next time we're downsizing' list.

■ Qualifications

When you're in education you're constantly working towards achieving qualifications, whether academic ones like GCSEs and A levels, or vocational ones like NVQs or Modern Apprenticeships. Your family and teachers tell you they're vitally important – and they are right. There's absolutely no doubt that you need to achieve the very best results you can in order to keep your options as wide as possible. But, and it's a crucial 'but', you will need more than good qualifications to impress a potential employer.

Schools and colleges are turning out more well-qualified applicants than ever before. The pass rate for A levels has gone up for 21 years in a row and now stands at over 95 per cent (2003). And more pupils than ever before are achieving A grades – over 21 per cent of them in 2003. When you realize that in 1970 the figure was just under 9 per cent, you can see how this makes life difficult for employers and admissions tutors, like Bill Swaddling of Brasenose College, Oxford. When the results came out in 2003 he told Radio 4's *Today* programme, 'A levels are no longer telling us which are the top students.'

The same goes for graduates. A first-class degree used to mark job-hunters out as exceptionally bright. It still does, but the fact is that employers had about 10,000 more graduates with firsts to choose from in 2001 than they did in 1995. Just to add to the confusion, the proportion of firsts awarded by universities varies widely as well. For example, in 2000 Cambridge University awarded firsts to nearly a third of its students, while other universities limited firsts to just 15 per cent of theirs. In its defence, Cambridge argues that top universities attract the best school-leavers and so naturally achieve the best degree results.

Young people may be working harder than ever before, examiners may be giving higher marks, exams may be getting easier – the debate rages on and you'll have to make your own mind up about what's going on. What matters to you right now is that employers (and universities) are less impressed by A grades and first-class degrees than they used to be.

Some universities are taking matters into their own hands. At the time of writing, eight universities, including Birmingham, Bristol, Cambridge, Durham, East Anglia, Nottingham, Oxford and University College London, are introducing a two-hour written exam in November 2004 for those who are applying to study law because so many of their applicants have top A-level grades. For example, about 4,000 school-leavers apply for 150 law places each year at UCL, and more than a third of them have three As or better at A level. The universities argue that results like that make it impossible to choose between candidates.

This could prove to be the start of a trend. If the universities find the tests do help them to pick out the best candidates, testing might be extended to candidates for other degree courses and at other universities in the future.

▓ Faces that fit

If you think about recruitment from the point of view of an employer trying to find the right person for the job, you can begin to see the problem. It has become extremely difficult to identify the best people purely from their exam results. You may leave education with an impressive array of certificates, but so will thousands of others.

IBM is one of a number of employers who may now ask to see graduates' A-level results, which are felt to be a better guide than the degree applicants have achieved. Young people wanting to become doctors may be put through specially designed tests to weed out 'unsuitable' candidates.

In fact, employers everywhere are increasingly using aptitude and personality tests to help them distinguish between candidates. Different employers favour different tests, but three out of every four job-seekers is now asked to undergo some form of assessment as well as an interview.

The tests you might be asked to do could range from filling in a form about your likes and dislikes to performing karaoke or line-dancing with a bunch of other hopeful job-hunters. (No, we're not joking.) Potential recruits have been asked to do all sorts of things from building Lego towers to being imprisoned under close observation in the *Big Brother* house.

However, you won't be surprised to hear that junior staff tend to get the more straightforward (and cheaper) exercises. Employers are likely to ask you to take further tests later in your career to help them assess your suitability for more senior roles that involve managing other people or shouldering major responsibilities.

By using tests, employers hope to identify people with initiative and leadership skills, though opinions vary about how effective testing is. Many employers tend to use similar test questions for recruiting junior staff. That means smart applicants can quickly pick up on what recruiters want to hear and go into interviews equipped with a mental list of the 'right' things to say to maximize their chances of getting the job.

Testing experts claim that it's a lot harder than it looks to fake your results, and if you are tempted to answer the questions less than honestly it's worth remembering that the whole point of the process is to find the right person for the right job. There's not a lot of point trying to convince an employer that you're ideal for a role that in reality won't suit you at all. You might end up with a job but the chances are you'll be looking for another one in a few months. Take the tests seriously and make sure you get some proper feedback about both the results and your interview. That way you'll gain valuable information about the impressions you're making on potential employers and be able to adjust your approach if you need to.

Team players

One of the criticisms of testing is that it can lead to organizations recruiting the same type of person over and over again. But that's precisely what some of them want to do because they believe that recruiting people in their own image builds a strong spirit of cooperation and loyalty. They actively set out to recruit people who fit the 'company mould', not just in terms of how they approach their work but also in terms of how they spend their time out of hours. Team drinks, inter-departmental get-togethers, sports clubs, family days, parties – employers use all sorts of methods in their attempts to encourage staff to bond.

As a rule, larger organizations tend to be keener on organized social events (they worry that staff from different parts of the business don't set eyes on each other from one month to the next and so can't interact effectively), and you can find that non-attendance is frowned upon.

You may like – or at least be comfortable with – the idea of socializing regularly with your workmates, or you may feel strongly that you'd prefer to draw a dividing line between work and home life. Either way, it's a good area to discuss with any potential boss.

Lack of skills

The good news – from your point of view – is that employers constantly complain they can't find good people. According to the CIPD, the second biggest problem employers run into in recruitment is poor quality applicants. But it's worth remembering that part of the reason for this could be people applying for jobs they're not qualified or suitable for, so you need to be realistic before you put yourself forward.

Now the bad news. On the whole, employers don't seem to think much of the young people coming out of school and university. The fact that people are leaving with more higher-grade qualifications doesn't seem to impress them either. A third of private-sector employers say they're not happy with basic literacy and numeracy skills among school-leavers, and the majority of them say that low levels of business awareness and poor self-management are a major problem among graduates and even more so among school-leavers.

Unfortunately there seems to be a mismatch between the skills that employers complain are in short supply and those that undergraduates think they need to brush up on. Here's a list of the skills that 1,000 students felt they needed to improve when they were surveyed in 2003.

SKILLS TO IMPROVE ON (STUDENTS' VIEW)

Presentation 55%	Communication 37%
Negotiation 48%	Time management 28%
Project management 45%	Teamwork 25%
Sales and marketing 37%	

CRAC 2003 survey of 1,000 undergraduates in various disciplines

They're all useful but – with the exception of the last two – they're not the skills most employers think are the problem areas. So be honest with yourself about your basic skills before you work on more sophisticated ones. There's no point honing your presentation skills if you can't write a decent business letter.

■ Foundation skills

So what are the basic skills you'll need to do your job? Whatever sort of work you want to do, American Professor Lawrence Jones believes that you need 17 'foundation skills' to do it as well as possible. The skills divide into four groups:

BASIC SKILLS Reading, writing, mathematics, speaking, listening.

THINKING SKILLS Creative thinking, problem-solving, decision-making, visualization (such as imagining how a system might work by looking at a diagram).

PEOPLE SKILLS Social, negotiation, leadership, teamwork, cultural diversity (i.e. working well with people from different backgrounds).

PERSONAL QUALITIES Self-esteem, self-management, responsibility.

But which ones do bosses think are the most important? Here's what members of the bosses' organization the CBI say that they look for above all else when they're recruiting:

> positive attitude to work
> team-working, communication, problem-solving
> IT skills
> literacy and numeracy
> knowledge about chosen career
> foreign-language skills

Whether you're planning to go into work straight from school or after university, you need to equip yourself with as many work-related skills as possible so that you stand out from the competition. Recruitment professionals recommend that you take on part-time or holiday work and get some job experience in the field you're hoping to go into. By doing that you can show potential employers you have realistic expectations, you have started to develop skills and you can understand and follow instructions from a manager.

■ A good attitude

Bosses want self-starters who don't wait to be told what to do but teach themselves new tricks. As time goes by, there is an ever greater emphasis on putting people together in teams to solve problems and develop new products. In the past people got promotion by demonstrating their technical, administrative and decision-making abilities. Bosses picked out strong leaders who they thought could control the behaviour of other workers. Today's enlightened employers are not looking for control freaks – they want commitment freaks. They will pick out people who love to collaborate with others and show themselves willing to take on more responsibility.

This is good news for anyone who is young and keen. Your parents may have waited years for promotion. Now the best firms spot promising front-line workers and give them new responsibilities. Their philosophy is simple: highly committed workers create a high-performance, high-profit workplace.

▓ A diverse workforce

Bright employers understand that there are commercial and social advantages in having a workforce that reflects the wide range of people who now make up modern Britain. And although minority groups are still heavily under-represented – particularly in certain types of work – more employers than ever before are actively trying to recruit people who don't necessarily fit the old 'white, middle-class male' stereotype.

And there are laws in place to make sure that trend spreads. It's already illegal for employers to discriminate against job applicants on the grounds of sex, race, ethnic origin, disability, sexual orientation or faith, and in 2006 they'll be prohibited from discriminating against people on the grounds that they're too old or too young as well. As part of their drive to abide by the law and recruit a more diverse staff, many employers now have written equal opportunity or diversity policies. Larger firms are more likely to have one than smaller organizations. That doesn't necessarily mean small firms don't want to recruit fairly, but it does suggest they might pay less attention to personnel or 'human resources' issues.

Employers don't always live up to the standards they lay claim to in their recruitment brochures. If you want to work in an organization that pays more than lip service to diversity, don't be afraid to ask questions about the range of people already on the staff. Don't be fobbed off with lines like 'we're an equal-opportunities employer', or even '15 per cent of our staff belong to ethnic minority groups'. If you want to understand the company's philosophy, you need to know what sort of work those people are doing. Are they man-agers? Or cleaners? In this area, actions speak louder than words.

▓ Pet hates

It's not difficult to get your head around what employers want from their staff – just put yourself in their shoes. And it's equally easy to work out what rubs them up the wrong way. Employers' pet hates:

poor attenders

poor timekeepers

over-promisers

under-deliverers

buck-passers

liars

clock-watchers

People who:

are lazy

don't listen

are unwilling to learn

are inflexible

can't admit mistakes

don't learn from mistakes

won't take responsibility for their actions

disrupt their colleagues

In this chapter we've talked about the qualities and skills that most bosses look for. Obviously particular jobs call for specialist skills as well, which you'll have to learn along the way, and individual bosses have their individual likes and dislikes. During the course of your career you'll work for a whole bunch of people. Some will be excellent managers, other won't. Like you, they'll all have their strengths and weaknesses. But if you make a point of trying to understand what your boss's priorities are, you'll be well on the way to understanding what he or she wants from you. As in all relationships, clear communication is the key, and that's your responsibility as much as theirs.

■ Key points

- ■ Employers place enormous value on soft skills such as flexibility and team working.
- ■ Bosses are not like teachers – your boss may not be very focused on your interests or career prospects.
- ■ Staff who keep on acquiring new skills are highly valued.

'Every day I get up
and look through
the *Forbes* list of
the richest people
in America. If I'm
not there, I go
to work.'

Robert Orben

Chapter 10
Doing your own thing

In this chapter you will find:

❑ Why some people seem to be born entrepreneurs –
willing to take risks and work as long as it takes to
create profitable businesses

❑ How our quiz can help you find out if you share some
of the typical features of entrepreneurial types

❑ A checklist for aspiring entrepreneurs

It might be that having waded through the book this far, you have come to a momentous decision. You don't want to spend your time working for someone else. You want to try your hand at setting up your own business – and as soon as possible.

You are – or you think you might be – a budding entrepreneur. So what exactly is an entrepreneur? It's basically someone who sees an opportunity and then finds a way to exploit it – in other words, an entrepreneur is anyone who starts his or her own business venture.

Perhaps you already have some hobby, interest, craft or part-time work experience you might be able to transform into a nice little earner. It's sobering to think that once you have undergone more training or gone to university and then got settled into the comfort of a regular job, you might feel less inclined to break out, give up your regular salary and try something new. So it really is worth considering all this now, if you feel it's a road you might want to go down.

■ Some people are born to sell

It could be that you are already known for being a bit of an ace bike or computer repairer. You might have spotted a gap in the services on offer in a nearby town or down your local high street. Maybe you already exhibited some signs of business ambition at a young age – even if it did involve profiteering or minor extortion in the school playground. If that's the case, you are probably a born salesperson.

In the future, as the largest companies cut down on their recruitment of school-leavers, greater numbers of young people are likely to be thinking along the same lines. Recently, Howard Davies, the director of the London School of Economics and former chairman of the Financial Services Authority, wrote an important report about this for the government: *Enterprise and the Economy in the Classroom*. In it he drew attention to the steady increase in numbers of young people becoming self-employed or going to work for the smallest firms. As his research showed, business entrepreneurs have become role models – and increasing numbers of us see running our own show as an attractive career option.

If you are at school or college, you might be lucky enough to spend a few days gaining experience of enterprise – perhaps setting up and running a mini-company or trying your hand at specific projects such as design, marketing, pricing and selling. It's a good way of getting a small taste of some of the things you might have to do if you had your own business.

But as Howard Davies also pointed out in his report, less than a third of all young people get this kind of chance while they are at school. So if you are unsure of your potential or abilities, read the rest of this chapter, do the quiz, and start to find out if you might have what it takes.

▓ Following in the footsteps of giants

You hardly need us to remind you that turning a mere idea into profitable reality will require a very particular combination of imagination, nerve, dogged determination and staying power. You will also need start-up finance to get your business going – far more than you might have expected. Yet there are plenty of tales of success to inspire you – just take a look at the business section of any large bookshop.

If you stopped people in the street and asked them to name a famous business man or woman, the chances are they would not immediately name the head of the oil company BP, the pharmaceutical giant SmithKline Beecham or the chief executive of Vodafone. Most people would probably mention Sir Richard Branson, founder of the Virgin transport, retail and finance empire. They might think of Stelios Haji-Ioannou, founder of easyJet. These are perhaps Britain's best-known 'serial entrepreneurs'.

Sir Richard started his business career at the age of nine – growing Christmas trees. Unfortunately, rabbits ate them. Undeterred, he later moved into student publishing before graduating to the music and airline business.

The revered American investor Warren Buffett runs Berkshire Hathaway – one of the most profitable companies in the world. He also began his working life at a young age. He used to buy multi-packs of Coca-Cola, break them up and sell the individual drinks to friends. Even today, he says he sticks to making or distributing straightforward products – such as Coca-Cola – which he knows and understands.

■ Entrepreneurs are a breed apart

This is not to say, however, that all entrepreneurs are self-made, or people without the patience to study hard or go to university. Far from it. Stelios Haji-Ioannou was the son of a wealthy Greek shipping magnate and came to Britain to study at the London School of Economics. He then followed his first degree with another – an MSc in Shipping Trade and Finance at City University, now the Cass Business School.

What is true is that, more than ever before, you are unlikely to get far without doing bags of homework, preparing a convincing business plan (a document going over your projected finances) and building up sufficient specialist knowledge of the trade or field you want to enter. Large numbers of today's successful enterprises were set up by individuals who started working for someone else, then decided to go their own way. So you may need to bide your time while you build up expertise and experience.

The national network of Business Link centres are a good place to get business start-up information in England – or there's Business Eye in Wales, Business Gateway and Highlands & Islands Enterprise in Scotland and Invest Northern Ireland in Belfast.

■ Do you have the entrepreneurial gene?

A good general business education at university or college could put you on the right road to running your own show, and time spent doing that is unlikely to be wasted. But while you can learn what makes a highly profitable business, you still need to have the right spark to create one yourself. Some people are convinced you have to be born with an 'entrepreneurial gene'. If your parents run a thriving business, it does not necessarily follow that you will have the same talent. Equally, you might be the first in your family with the desire to branch out on your own.

What is true is that if you have practical skills and decide to turn them into a business, hairdressing or plumbing abilities are as likely to put you on Millionaire's Row as a university degree, rich parents or a previous professional career. Many of Britain's wealthiest people made their fortunes on the back of what they learnt studying for a trade qualification or apprenticeship.

Each year, the *Sunday Times* produces a Rich List. A substantial number of the successful business men and women on it are so-called 'craft millionaires'. These are practical people who have not only excelled in their chosen trade and become independently wealthy, but have also, in some cases, become celebrities. People such as the fashion designer Alexander McQueen, the hairdresser John Frieda or TV gardener Alan Titchmarsh.

Among the wealthiest craftsmen are the leisure entrepreneur Trevor Hemmings, worth an estimated £480m, and fashion designer Karen Millen. She started selling shirts from her parents' house after a fashion course and now runs a chain of 50 stores in the UK.

But the top slot in the special list of craft millionaires (at the time of writing) is held by the Phones 4U founder John Caudwell, who quit school after just one term of A levels and began his career as an apprentice at the Michelin Tyre Company. He is now worth an estimated £840m.

THE RICH LIST

John Caudwell	mobile phones	£840m
Trevor Hemmings	leisure and property	£480m
Jim McColl	industry (Clyde Blowers)	£305m
John Frieda	hairdressing	£167m
Laurence Graff	diamonds	£157m
Jack Tordoff	car sales	£85m
Peter Dawson	truck hire	£82m
Sir Stan Clarke	racecourses & property	£80m
Robbie Cowling	internet	£75m
Kevin McDonald	industry	£75m

Vocational Rich List 2003, compiled by Philip Beresford for City and Guilds

■ Entrepreneurs are everywhere

You might think it's all very well for a handful of now legendary business types who got lucky many years ago. Yet there are thousands of recent, down-to-earth examples of people who have made enormous strides from small beginnings. Here are just a few.

Still in her early twenties, **Sharon Hill** is often described as one of Swindon's youngest entrepreneurs. She's a founder of Creative Communication – an internet marketing and web design company she set up with a partner at Swindon in Wiltshire. Sharon's first venture into entrepreneurial waters was selling cross-stitch cards at local markets to raise extra pocket money. But she did have a role model – her parents had their own business – so it was no great surprise to family and friends when she began making plans to set up on her own. Sharon trained to be an ice-skater in France and it was there that she went to work for a wine company and got involved in marketing their products on the internet. Five years later, she had set up on her own back in the UK. Sharon says she is always running into older people who say she's so lucky to have her own business and they only wish they'd had the courage to do the same years ago.

'You only have one life – so why not take the chance? It can be lonely when you start out on your own, but I have no regrets. The personal satisfaction you get from running your own company makes everything worth it.'

Nasa Khan has been described as one of the UK's leading young business visionaries, and at the age of 30 he's already one of Britain's top Asian millionaires. He started his own business just eight years ago with £2,000 of his own money. The Accessory People is now a market-leader – making and distributing accessories for cellular phones and computers. It has an annual turnover of £450 million and employs 50 people.

Nasa was an economics student at Kingston University and says it was this that laid the foundations of his success. 'Economics gave me an understanding of the world. It explains why people behave the way they do. The atmosphere was great – lecturers were inspiring and helpful, and the environment was friendly and pleasant,' he said. 'I learned the value of reputation at Kingston and I've tried to create that same sense of ownership among staff and clients at The Accessory People.'

Wedding-dress designer **Tara Wilkinson** of Wingate in County Durham got started with financial help and business advice from The Prince's Trust. Her business is thriving after three years of trading and the future looks good. Tara

Wilkinson's first small shop Exclusively Yours was opened in 2000, thanks to a Prince's Trust loan and a grant from the European Regional Development Fund. She has since moved into larger premises that she designed herself, complete with showrooms and workrooms. Tara designs and makes custom-fitted wedding and bridesmaids' dresses and her service is so popular she has a month-long waiting list for appointments. Tara now has four employees to help with the business.

The Prince's Trust business manager for Durham, Brenda Baxter, says: 'Tara is a shining example of a new business start which is not only surviving, but expanding, too. That's all down to her enthusiasm, drive, creative talent and her amazing capacity for hard work.' The Prince's Trust helps over 4,000 young people each year with start-up finance and support. For information call 0800 842842 or visit www.princes-trust.org.uk.

If you are thinking of taking the plunge, it's crucial to think about where the money to start your new business will come from – you really do have to plan every aspect of your finances thoroughly. According to the business credit specialists Dun & Bradstreet, nine out of ten of all small business failures can be put down to insufficient funding, poor management and lack of planning.

Do what you like and get paid for it

Lots of people in the middle of their careers decide to jack it all in and switch to something they really enjoy. So why not start by doing what you like in the first place? It could be that your favourite interests, hobbies or spare-time activities might hold the key to your future.

When you start to think about it, almost everything we spend our time doing involves handing over money for goods or services. You might enjoy going to cafés, caring for animals, listening to particular styles of music, playing with computers, building things or working part time in a hairdresser's or beauty salon. It's also worth thinking more laterally about the things you are passionate about. For example, if you are a serious football, cricket, golf or tennis fan, you might not make the national or local team, but how about working in or even setting up a sports store, or looking at some of the many opportunities now open in the leisure field?

The important thing here is that you would be meeting or working with people with similar interests, and your enthusiasm and knowledge would hopefully come over well to your customers and provide a good basis from which to start building a business or career.

Even if you are not focusing on starting your own business, hobbies might also give you a clue as to what you have an aptitude for. For example, if you like tinkering with cars, perhaps you should find out more about opportunities in engineering. If you find you are good at caring for people, then it would be worth exploring the social services or health sector. Perhaps you enjoy reading the City pages, or predicting the movements of quoted companies or currencies. In that case, why not explore the idea of playing the markets professionally by looking at a career in banking or finance? Alternatively, there might be nothing you like better than a good argument – in which case you might be perfectly suited to becoming a barrister or solicitor.

■ Going pro

One of the difficult dilemmas that can face talented people is whether or not they should try to make a career out of what they love doing. We're talking here about those with the potential to become professional musicians, dancers, actors, artists or sportsmen and women. For such people, it's usually all or nothing – settling for work in a related field would be pretty unattractive.

It's an area where parents can become especially anxious, worrying about what might happen if such a career is short-lived, or never gets off the ground. No one can make such a decision for you. But it does make sense to take constant advice from your coach, your teachers or tutors. Ask them if they really feel you have what it takes to get to the very top. If so, what would you have to do – or give up – in order to get there?

■ Are you a self-starter?

Talent and a great idea will help you get started, but remember you do have to be a self-starter. Most successful entrepreneurs are resourceful and energetic. They like to solve problems and have the ability to make confident decisions.

Often they are born leaders who can inspire, persuade and motivate others. They are also versatile. Business owners need to wear lots of different hats.

So, could this be you in a few years' time? Let's find out.

QUIZ: DO YOU HAVE WHAT IT TAKES TO BE AN ENTREPRENEUR?

No quiz can ever tell you if you're cut out to be your own boss and well on your way to making your first million. But this one might help you see if you share some of the traits typical of an entrepreneur. Answer Yes or No to the questions. As always, there are no right or wrong answers. But be honest!

1 Do you start each day feeling positive?

2 When things go wrong, do you pick yourself up and try again?

3 Do you like yourself and who you are?

4 Do you like to make things happen rather than wait for them to happen?

5 Do you easily get discouraged if things don't go to plan?

6 If you do something different do you worry about what others will think?

7 Are you a good salesperson? Can you sell your ideas to others?

8 Can you get along with people you don't like?

9 Are you a good judge of character – could you hire (and fire) the right people if you wanted to expand your business?

10 Does pressure feed you rather than get to you?

11 Do you observe what is happening around you, and have a sixth sense for what people want?

12 Do you usually learn from your mistakes?

13 Are you a good organizer?

14 Do you look for better ways to do things – for example, while doing this test, are you thinking of ways to make it better?

15 As a child, were you always finding ways of making money?

16 Do you have family or friends who could help you get started, ideally who have small-business experience?

17 Do you have the ability to think through possible outcomes – and take steps to ensure they do, or don't, happen?

18 Can you make quick decisions and feel comfortable about them afterwards?

19 Do you relate well to people of different backgrounds?

20 Can you start a conversation if you find yourself in a room full of strangers?

21 Can you express yourself well, so people are interested in what you are talking about?

22 Do you keep to deadlines you have been set?

23 When you start something, do you see it through?

24 Can you manage to juggle several projects at the same time?

25 In a discussion, can you persuade people to change their minds by the force of your arguments?

26 Are you comfortable talking to groups of people?

27 Do you read the business pages and keep up with current affairs?

28 Do you know the difference between gross and net profits?

29 Do you understand terms like assets, liabilities, goodwill and working capital – or are you interested in finding out?

30 Would you be happy to ring strangers or knock at their doors and try to sell them things?

31 Are you willing to work long hours and go without holidays?

32 If you have any savings, would you be willing to invest and possibly lose a large proportion of them?

33 Would you be prepared to accept a lower standard of living until your business became profitable?

34 Do you have a strong feeling one day you'll be personally successful?

35 Do you feel a need to achieve something on your own?

36 Are you sometimes uncomfortable with authority?

37 Do people sometimes think you are a bit of a chancer?

38 Do you tend to have stronger opinions than your friends?

39 Can you easily discard or change your plans when circumstances dictate?

40 Do you quickly get bored unless you can control your own work?

SCORING

Give yourself one point for every 'yes'.

If you scored 30 or more

On the face of it, you have many of the characteristics of a self-made business person. You like to look at possibilities, make your own decisions and change direction as necessary to achieve your goals.

If you scored 20–30 points

You have some but not all the qualities of a successful entrepreneur. Have a look at what follows this quiz to see if you can spot any of your potential weaknesses. If you're still keen to be the next Sir Richard Branson, you could start trying to make up for any deficiencies by retraining yourself. Comfort yourself with the thought that once your new business is doing well, you can hire people with the skills or the patience you think you lack.

Under 20 points

Being an entrepreneur may not be for you. Running your own business involves lots of hassle, so maybe you'd be happier in a more secure job, working for someone else who can take the risks.

■ Entrepreneurs are a special breed

Over the years, lots of studies have been made of people who run their own businesses. Researchers like to look at groups of people who do similar things in life – to see if they share any common characteristics.

One interesting finding here was that people who start their own businesses often have strong opinions – and not just about their own work. It could be about their football team, religion, economics or local issues – it doesn't really matter what. If you think about it, it makes a lot of sense. If you are going to risk your time and money in your own venture, you must have a strong conviction that it is going to succeed.

Sometimes it helps to work with someone who has a different outlook. Brent Hoberman, the founder of lastminute.com, the online travel and entertainment website, was always totally convinced that an internet company selling unsold plane and theatre tickets would make a fantastic business. His former partner in the project, Martha Lane-Fox, was less sure about the idea, but gave it her best shot. The combination of unbridled enthusiasm and practicality worked brilliantly. Together, they grew the business and were soon taking it public on the stock market – only to see the dot.com bubble burst and the value of their shares plunge to almost nothing. Yet they kept their nerve and were able to overcome huge setbacks to rebuild the business, which is now by far the largest travel operator of its kind.

Entrepreneurs often seem to be the kind of people who most resent being told what to do by others – they tend to be uncomfortable working for other bosses, and may have got into trouble at home or at school. Another feature of many entrepreneurs is that they have a strong 'need for achievement' – they have great self-motivation. What's a good decision for an entrepreneur would be a gamble or a risk for the rest of us. For better or worse, people who run their own businesses often fail to see the pitfalls that others see straight away. On the positive side, this means they sometimes achieve the apparently impossible. But they also rush in where angels fear to tread, as the saying goes.

So if you answered 'yes' to most of the questions, and you are definitely up for starting a business, you will need to stick with it. Just think about some of the much-publicized problems that, say, Virgin or easyJet have encountered along the way. Sir Richard Branson would be the first to admit that he does not always strike gold.

■ So you think you'd make a great entrepreneur
Among the qualities you will need are:

- ■ **Drive** – demonstrated by your self-motivation, vigour, initiative, good health, persistence and the ability to take responsibility for your actions.
- ■ **Thinking ability** – that's original, creative, critical and analytical thinking.
- ■ **People skills** – you will have to be sociable, considerate, cheerful, tactful and emotionally stable.

- **Communication skills** – writing, speaking, comprehending and responding appropriately to your customers.
- **Technical knowledge** – able to manage the actual manufacture or delivery of goods and services.

Checklist for aspiring entrepreneurs

Another good tip is to study why and how others have failed in business – so you don't make the same mistakes. Such experiences can teach us a great deal. Duncan Cheatle, a 'business doctor' and founder of the advisory organization Prelude2Business, has come up with these top ten tips for people who want to run their own business.

- **Do it for passion, not money**. Things don't happen overnight, so do something you feel passionate about. Do not start something with an exit and a fortune in mind. You'll probably fail. This was commonplace during the dot.com era where people came up with ludicrous business ideas.
- **Do something you know about.** Philip Green, the retail entrepreneur, gave this advice. He and his family only invest in retail businesses, because that's what they understand. If you go into something you know little or nothing about, you will soon be out of your depth.
- **Don't give up too early.** Successful businesses are usually different from those described in their original business plan. Try something and, if it isn't working, try it a different way.
- **Have a mentor.** First-time entrepreneurs often fail because they don't have someone experienced they can turn to for advice as things come up. Everyone needs a sounding board.
- **Get the funding right**. Businesses often spend too much time chasing the wrong form of funding from the wrong people. It can take a long time to get people to pay you.
- **Manage your money well.** Ensure you have financial plans and see if you are keeping to them.
- **Build sales before anything else.** A lot of people spend too much

time getting things such as a nice office and the website sorted instead of getting out there and making sales.

- **Don't try to rush.** Winning customers takes time – sell, tweak what you are offering, then sell again.
- **Be wary of bad advice.** Friends may mean well, but they can lead you astray.
- **Keep things flexible.** You don't want to get locked into anything you can't get out of easily and cheaply – like taking on more staff.

Key points

- Many successful people who have started their own businesses have vocational qualifications, but may not have been to university.
- It's usually best to build up expertise in your chosen field and get help to prepare a proper business plan before taking the plunge.
- Look for entrepreneurial leanings in your past and current activities.
- Do some more background reading – there are loads of success stories to inspire you and to learn from.

'I am a strong believer in luck, and I find the harder I work, the more I have of it.'

Benjamin Franklin
(1706–1790)

Chapter 11
Decisions, decisions

In this chapter you will find:

❏ How your subject options should relate to your career
plans whenever possible

❏ Vocational training vs university: which is right for you

❏ What's involved in taking a gap year before
further study

❏ What your style of learning is

Whether or not you have a particular career in mind, the first important choices you face are at age 13 or 14 in Year 9 at secondary school. That's when you pick your GCSE subjects to study in Years 10 and 11. Making these choices is not always easy, so make sure you get lots of help. This really is the time to start talking to teachers, careers advisers, friends and – most of all – your parents. They know your strengths and weaknesses and can help to crystallize your thoughts.

For a start, English, maths and a science are compulsory. As to what other subjects you should choose, the best advice is to work out what you think you might need for your future and combine those subjects with others you enjoy and are good at. If at all possible, your options should include a balance of arts, sciences, languages and technological and creative subjects.

Don't make the mistake of choosing subjects just because your friends are doing them. You might like the idea of being in the same classes as your mates but that shouldn't be your first priority. Don't be afraid to be different – teachers and parents will be impressed by your maturity, and when exam time comes along you'll be glad you focused on subjects that were right for you.

If you are truly turned off by academic study, it might be possible to start some job training when you are 14 – two years before the official school-leaving age. So called 'vocational' GCSEs are being set up, allowing you to spend two days (unpaid) as a junior apprentice in a range of trades including plumbing, carpentry, car mechanics and bricklaying. The rest of the time would be spent in school or college. Similar schemes may be offered in the future in some places in subjects such as business, leisure and tourism. The hope is that, if your placements work out well, you might want to continue your education in your chosen trade rather than dropping out without any useful qualifications or skills. But don't start celebrating if you can't wait to leave the classroom – you still can't actually leave school at 14.

■ More choices at 16

You're 16 and in the last of no less than 12 years of compulsory schooling. It's at this point that you have to make decisions that will have an impact on your adult life. If you find that idea daunting, try thinking about it this way – you're finally getting the chance to start putting your ideas about how you want to shape your life into practice, and that's got to be a good thing. You could:

- Stay on at school (or go to sixth-form college) and study A levels, start on a course for an Advanced Vocational Certificate of Education (AVCE), or do a mixture of both
- Study at a further education college – often with a job area in mind
- Get a job, preferably with training – such as a Modern Apprenticeship

Of course, these choices will be easier to make if you have career ideas in mind.

All change – and not for the first time

Keeping up with the latest exam and training options is practically a vocation in itself. No wonder careers teachers sometimes look harassed. As it is, changes have been taking place under the general heading of Curriculum 2000 – changes designed to allow easier combinations of academic and vocational study for 16- to 19-year-olds. Why shouldn't you mix and match if you want to?

More recently, the former chief inspector of schools, Mike Tomlinson, has been commissioned by the government to take things further. He has come up with a grander, long-term plan to absorb GCSEs and A levels into a new four-tier diploma scheme. It's a mixed bag of proposals, which has not received a universal welcome – especially from teachers. Things are definitely moving in the direction of a broader-based approach, putting work-related training on a more equal footing with traditional learning.

As the National Association of Head Teachers has pointed out, the trend is towards a style of education closer to that promoted by the much-admired International Baccalaureate Organization – a not-for-profit educational foundation with its headquarters in Geneva, Switzerland. Some schools offer its two-year courses in the UK as an alternative to A levels. They are now available in 116 countries, but are most popular in continental Europe. Students study a wider range of subjects, some of them in depth – an approach that can provide especially good preparation for university.

■ Know what you are letting yourself in for

If A levels and university entry are part of your plans, you need to understand what you are letting yourself in for. A survey carried out in 2003 found as many as half of the teenagers surveyed believed they might have made the wrong choice of GCSE and A-level subjects. Of the AS and A-level students, more than a quarter questioned weren't sure of completing at least one of their subjects.

So what's going wrong? Why are so many students finding they might not have made the best subject choices? According to the survey, the problem seemed to be that most of the pupils concerned found their course work was harder than they had expected. Worryingly, half of them said they had lost confidence in their own abilities as a result.

AS-level exams have not been an unqualified success. One of the objectives in introducing them was to encourage the study of a wider range of subjects. This gives you more time to find out what you are good at before you make final choices for the second and final year at A level, but the problem has been the burden on some students, who felt under too much pressure.

Whatever changes may be introduced in the future, it is always a good plan to find out exactly what each subject syllabus covers, and what will be tested and when. What you don't want is to be put off a subject because the workload comes as a surprise. Forewarned is forearmed. If you do make a mistake it's hardly the end of the world, but you don't want to dent your confidence when you're just getting started at college or in the sixth form.

■ University is not for everyone

As you study for your A levels, you will soon find it's make-your-mind-up time once again. The big change in recent years has been a vast increase in the numbers of people going on from school to further (college) and higher (university) education.

As recently as 1985, only around 40 per cent of young people chose further education. Now nearly twice as many do so, and the government is not far off achieving its target of getting half of all 18-year-olds into university every year. These figures go some way towards explaining why those who do opt for a job or work-based training are sometimes made to feel like second-class citizens. Higher education has almost become accepted as the 'best' option for everyone regardless of their personal ideas and abilities. By comparison, Modern Apprenticeships and other vocational courses are viewed by some as a choice for lower-achievers or those who have failed their exams. In short, they have an image problem – and that's a pity. It's also a pity that in some areas the availability of Modern Apprenticeships falls short of what it should be.

Teachers who give careers advice as part of their teaching role are not always well informed about what work-based education has to offer. Many schools do have a vested financial interest in hanging onto students for their own sixth forms. In a survey of apprentices, two-thirds said they were advised by their teachers to stay in full-time education, even though half of them wanted to start their training at 16. Some reckoned the advice they were given was a little biased towards what the school wanted, rather than what might have been best for them.

■ Balancing ambition with reality

If your dream career depends on top academic achievement and you have the ability, you can rest assured that your parents and teachers will almost certainly encourage and push you. Schools want to make a good showing in the league tables. Most parents want their kids to achieve more than they did.

But get real. There's no point in thinking you will make it as a merchant banker if you repeatedly failed at maths and the very idea of spending time wading through figures bores you rigid. Equally, if you struggle with science you are unlikely to achieve your lifelong ambition to be a pilot. Look instead for alternative ways to enter the financial sector, or investigate the wide variety of work offered by the airline industry.

Studies by FOCUS, the Central London Training and Enterprise Council, suggest that the idea that work-based career training is second best can have some unfortunate side effects. FOCUS found that too many young people steer clear of Modern Apprenticeships and stick with academic studies. But they often have unrealistic expectations about their exam results. Then they flounder and are shocked to learn that they might not make the grade and win the college or university place they are banking on. So after a wasteful and soul-destroying time, they have to start all over again. Meanwhile, their mates who made different choices are forging ahead getting qualifications – and earning themselves a wage into the bargain.

■ Vocational training makes a comeback

It does appear that the pendulum is starting to swing back towards work-based training. National politicians, business organizations and educationalists are all starting to question the point – and the cost – of spending three years on some of today's university courses.

A study by Warwick University's Institute for Employment Studies predicts that by 2010 there may be 2.3 million more people with degrees than there were in 1999. It also forecasts over 2 million new jobs will be created.

That sounds pretty good. Yet this research has a sting in its tail because the team that carried it out reckons that less than half of these new jobs will be in the kind of highly paid 'professional occupations' that graduates tend to aim for. As the number of graduates continues to rise, qualified people are increasingly taking jobs outside the traditional areas of graduate employment because there aren't enough top posts to go round, and that trend looks set to continue.

However, this does not mean you will be wasting your time if you decide to continue your education. It's still going to be the poorly educated or under-trained people who end up in the worst jobs. But you shouldn't feel that continuing to learn has to mean going to university.

■ 'We need bright young people now!'

If training on the job appeals, look no further than Britain's small and medium-sized businesses. More than 135,000 are represented by the British Chambers of Commerce. As Isabella Moore, the BCC president, put it after another bumper crop of exam results: 'Businesses need bright young people now. Successful students need not follow the crowd to university to do well in life. In a productive economy, there must be a technical engineer for every public relations professional, a small business owner for every management consultant. Today young people have many choices. They should consider the profitable opportunities of becoming entrepreneurs or taking on a modern apprenticeship.'

The national chairman of the Federation of Small Businesses, John Emmins, makes a similar point: 'After three years of exams, A-level students can feel like they are on a production line with university and conventional employment the next steps in the process. But the world of work has changed significantly over the last few years and young people really do have a choice. More and more people, at different stages in their lives, are seeing self-employment as the more attractive option.' (See Chapter 10 on Doing Your Own Thing.)

■ Learning for 'hands on' people

Vocational courses are geared up to lead to a particular type of work. Some are for those who know the broad area they want to specialize in, but not the exact role. Others prepare you for one particular job.

There's a bewildering range of qualifications you can go for – but like university degrees, they are not all the same and some will carry more weight than others. So if you do have a particular job or potential employer in mind, it's worth doing some research to see what value the employer places on a particular qualification. Here are just a few:

- **General National Vocational Qualifications (GNVQs)** and **Vocational A Levels** are probably the best known of the job-related courses and can lead on to work or to a higher qualification. They allow you to study broad work areas: leisure and tourism, science, manufacturing, retail and distribution, art and design, hospitality and catering, health and social care, performing arts, engineering, media, business studies, the built environment and IT.
- **National Qualifications** can also lead to employment or higher education. They tend to be more specialized – for example, you can study nursery nursing, design or beauty therapy.

■ **National Vocational Qualifications (NVQs)** go to people who are already working and want to get a qualification, or for people who know exactly what work they want to train for.
■ **Other Courses**. There are many more to choose from – BTEC First Diplomas, SVQs in Scotland, and qualifications awarded by organizations such as City and Guilds, RSA and Edexcel. Connexions and careers libraries should be able to help with more information.

Most of these courses are studied in colleges of education, but some will increasingly be offered by schools alongside traditional subjects.

■ Modern Apprenticeships

Another alternative worth considering – especially if earning money is important – is a Modern Apprenticeship. Anyone over 16 can apply for one. You learn on the job, building up knowledge and skills, and gaining qualifications and a wage all at the same time. There are two levels of Modern Apprenticeship: Foundation (FMA) and Advanced (AMA). Both can lead to National Vocational Qualifications (NVQs), key skills qualifications and technical certificates.

In the year to 2003, 452 young people became modern apprentices. The government is aiming for over 46,000 16- to 25-year-olds starting in 2005.

The apprenticeships cover a wide range of business sectors, including administration, construction, manufacturing, health, recreation and transport – in theory. Unfortunately, one of the big problems with Modern Apprenticeships is that what is available to you depends very much on where you live. The system relies on getting local employers on board, and in many parts of the country that's proved a major problem. So before you sell yourself the idea of an MA, check out what's on offer in your area and – crucially – the quality of the training you could expect if you signed up.

The drop-out rate is high in some subjects, although, interestingly, research has shown even those who don't stay the course do usually find work, perhaps because of the skills they have learnt. In some areas, the quality of the training offered by these apprenticeships has been criticized by the Adult Learning Inspectorate, which oversees them. Efforts are underway to raise the standards, but meanwhile you would be best advised to establish exactly what a particular apprenticeship offers before you sign up for it. In the meantime, the inspectorate reports that the best programmes are currently most likely to be found in business administration, care and engineering.

And if you're still worrying about that 'second best' tag, think again. Nearly 60 per cent of the engineering apprentices in one study had at least 8 GCSEs and almost a quarter had at least one A level. The majority were also considering further qualifications, including a degree – though most wanted to get them by studying part time while continuing to work. So Modern Apprenticeships aren't for people who can't do exams; they are for people who don't feel they're suited to full-time education.

▒ Opting for university

If you're sure a degree is the right thing for you, think carefully about which courses you apply for. Get as much information as possible from all the sources we talk about in this book – careers advisers, family, friends and the universities themselves – before you take the plunge. Talk to students doing the courses you have in mind and ask about the subject, the teaching staff and the work involved, and what they like/dislike about the way the syllabus is taught.

One new and alternative route into higher education worth considering is the growing range of two-year foundation degrees. These courses are very much in the new spirit of marrying work-based training with relevant academic studies. They aim to help meet the shortage of skilled workers in industry – so if you do well there's a great chance of a job at the end. Subjects on offer in various parts of the country range from aircraft engineering to health and social care and police studies.

▒ It's going to cost you – or your parents

You will almost certainly leave university with debts – how big they are will depend on how much financial help your family give you, the number of years that you study for and the decisions you take about your finances while you're a student. These might include whether you work during term-time and vacations and how well you manage your weekly budget. And by the way, if you're relying on your parents to pick up the bills, you should know that only about six in every 10 families are currently saving towards their children's higher education. Of these, a third are putting away less than £300 a year.

The way higher education is funded is changing and predictions vary widely as to how big student debts may be in the future. However, the fact remains that going to university is an expensive business. With that in mind you don't want to start a course only to find that it's not the right one – so give yourself plenty of time for research before you make your choice.

Students frequently drop out. This may be for academic, personal or financial reasons, but according to the admissions service UCAS, one of the most common reasons is that courses do not turn out as expected. Yet another reason to do your research first.

It's also partly why UCAS has launched a new service to give applicants more information about the courses they want to study and an insight into what admissions tutors are looking for besides exam results when they offer places. Admissions Criteria Profiles, as they're known, will be available for thousands of courses over the next few years and you can find them through the course search on the UCAS website.

▨ Non-vocational degrees

If you're thinking of doing a non-vocational degree (that is, one that won't directly prepare you for going into a particular line of work, such as law or medicine), you need to think about the financial implications. That is not to say that you should turn your back on degree subjects that aim to develop your knowledge and understanding rather than train you to do a job of work. Where would society be without philosophers, historians, classics scholars and all the rest of those people who pursue knowledge for its own sake? Considerably worse off is undoubtedly the answer to that question – but there's no denying that the same could go for your bank balance if you choose to follow in their footsteps.

Contrary to what you may have read or been told, your time at university – if you choose to go – does not necessarily have to be about preparing you for a lucrative career. Use it for that purpose if you want to, but don't be afraid to reject that idea in favour of a more academic approach. Studying for a degree offers a rare and valuable opportunity for intellectual exploration and growth. As long as you've thoroughly researched the course you want to do, you should not let financial worries put you off. You're unlikely to have such an opportunity again.

Of course, there's no reason why you shouldn't do a non-vocational degree and then pursue a mainstream job. Just because you spend three years deciphering ancient languages doesn't mean that you have to spend your whole career doing the same thing. You can always go on to train for a career in law or business or whatever afterwards if you want to. But if you find that three years of really using your brain has given you a taste for doing so, then you'll probably be happier finding a job that lets you do that, rather than pursuing a purely commercial career. While it's generally true that jobs where you don't generate money for your employer don't tend to pay well, there is more to enjoying working life than a fat pay cheque.

If you want to stretch your brain even further, think about postgraduate education – studying for a masters or a doctorate qualification after finishing your degree. This can take a number of years and involve you in considerable expense. Even if you leave university as soon as you've gained your first degree in a highly academic subject, you might find it more difficult to get a job than friends with degrees employers can immediately see a use for – such as law, computing or business studies. Employers often value practical skills and knowledge above intellectual accomplishment.

The main message here is to be practical – at least look at what your education is going to cost you and think realistically about how you're going to make a living and pay off your debts when you leave.

■ Applying to university

You might be sure about which course you want to do but you've still got to clear another big hurdle – impressing those all-powerful university admission tutors, who decide who can have a place and who can't.

Every year, applications from more than 400,000 people arrive with an electronic ping in the overstretched offices of UK universities. Most applicants will not get the chance to impress or plead their case in a personal interview.

So how do you make sure that it's not your UCAS form that gets left on the shelf by the admissions staff – leaving you without the offers you need? There's no mystery here. You simply have to persuade the tutors that you have what it takes – that you are the best of the bunch of applicants chasing a limited number of places. So, ultimately, it all hangs on what are sometimes described as 'the big three': your personal statement, your qualifications and your reference.

Make it personal

Your personal statement is the one chance you have to stand out from the crowd. Admissions tutors often complain that what people write here is surprisingly impersonal – either that or applicants follow a formula taught to them at school that does not entirely ring true for them.

A strong, confident application will set out why you are choosing to do the courses that you are, and some particular reasons why you are interested. A clear understanding of what you have signed up for academically not only reduces the risk of three years doing something you hate, it is also one of the best ways to impress. After all, you are trying to convince academic staff that you are a suitable new recruit to the subject to which they have devoted their working life. Try not to waffle, but say more than just 'I enjoy this'.

Tutors also say there's no need to go over the top describing how you lived with yaks, or can play five different musical instruments. Ultimately, they want to sign people up who can show a sustained commitment to study. If you have been to one unusual place or done something that enthused and inspired you, it's going to prove more useful than a list of all the exotic holidays you have been on.

Put work ambitions in context

You might think you should play up your future employment plans – but it's not always best to overdo references to your career ambitions. Generally, the more academic your course, the more you may first need to explain why you want to spend three years reading about it in the library. Applicants for business or the professions are probably on safer ground setting out where they see themselves in the future. Admissions tutors are also looking for signs of maturity and responsibility, so if you have done some kind of a part-time job, this may demonstrate that you have management skills and can organize your time well.

And don't leave things until the final deadline

Theoretically, all applications will be considered on merit, but if tutors have already seen some great applications, it may take a lot to impress them.

▨ Gap years

For some, the road to the job of your dreams seems a long one. All those years at school and sixth form, at least another three at university – then the prospect of having to start at the bottom of the career ladder when you finally get a job.

Perhaps it's no wonder that around 7 per cent of all school-leavers who applied to university in 2002 deferred their entry in order to take a gap year. Taking a break of this kind used to be frowned on in many quarters. Now it's more widely recognized by admissions tutors and employers (and even parents) that a year off can be a valuable experience that can put you in a better position to continue your educational or work career afterwards.

Even the term 'gap year' can be confusing. Students often go travelling before entering university, but gap years can also be taken during or after your time at college. Nor is it just backpacking. Work, volunteering, work experience and study can all be fitted into a gap year.

You can take your gap year …

… **before higher education**. Start it when you finish A levels and you've got 15 months to follow your dream. You will need to defer your place at university. Alternatively, if you are taking time out to improve your grades, you can re-apply the following year.

… **during higher education**. This is sometimes described as a 'sandwich year'. Popular with those doing a masters degree – it's often used to get practical experience volunteering or doing fieldwork. This should be pre-arranged in good time with your university.

… **after higher education**. Some graduates choose to take time out between university and work because they like the idea of a break before they knuckle down to a job. Some (usually larger or public-sector) employers are prepared to offer graduate positions with a starting date deferred by six months or a year to allow their new recruits to take time out.

As to what you can do in your gap year, there are numerous guides and websites to inspire you and they're worth checking out for ideas you might not have thought of. Setting off to see the world with friends may never seem more appealing. But beware – if you don't have a private income you will need to work at some stage to pay for your plane ticket.

■ How do you like to learn?

If you can't make up your mind whether university or a work-based approach is for you, you might find it helpful to start by working out which style of learning suits you best.

Learning doesn't have to be 'formal', nor does it have to be full time. When you are at school, there's not usually much choice. You sit in class, teachers try to cram the entire National Curriculum into your brain, you make notes, contribute when asked to do so, and sit an exam at the end. If you choose carefully, you'll probably find further education a lot more fun than some of the stuff you're learning now because you will have far more say in how you do it.

For example, if you are a practical, hands-on person, your preferred way of learning may be different from that of some of your friends. If you simply followed the crowd, there is a risk that you could end up isolated or unskilled.

For example, have you ever found yourself saying:
- I've really tried concentrating, but this class is so boring …
- To be honest, I've felt lost all term.
- This isn't the kind of exam that I can do well in.
- She's obviously a good teacher, but her style doesn't suit me.
- My project would have been far better if I could have approached it in my own way.

Such comments reflect the wide variation in the ways we learn. There is no best way – we are just all different.

■ Try the flat-pack furniture test

We all do things differently – but in the end, the job gets done. Think for a moment about what you would do if you were to start building a new wardrobe for your bedroom – one of those that looks great in the brochure but arrives in a huge flat-pack with lots of mysterious-looking parts that all need fixing together.

Would you take your time to study the leaflet, lay out all the parts on the floor and work out the whole procedure before getting started? Perhaps you would ignore the badly translated instructions, start picking up the parts and figure it out for yourself by trial and error. Or would you call in someone else, a parent or friend perhaps, who might have tackled something similar before and could help you finish the job?

What determines your approach is your personal learning style – and experts have developed many theories about it. So, to get thinking about how you like to learn, why not take our quiz?

QUIZ: WHAT'S YOUR LEARNING STYLE?

To find out more about how you like to learn, tick the box against any of these 40 statements with which you agree or largely agree. If you disagree with any statement, leave the box blank and go on to the next one.

If you prefer not to mark your book, list the numbers 1 to 40 on a sheet of paper and put a tick against the numbers of the statements you agree with. Then follow the instructions at the end to see how to score your test. The exercise should take no longer than 10 minutes to complete. There are no right or wrong answers.

1 I often act without considering all the possible consequences ☐
2 It's really annoying when people start putting things together before reading the instructions. ☐
3 I take pride in doing a thorough job. ☐

4 I prefer jumping in and doing things spontaneously rather
   than planning them in advance. ☐

5 I find it quite difficult to come up with crazy ideas off the top
   of my head. ☐

6 I usually listen more than talk. ☐

7 I like to discover how things work. ☐

8 I'm fussy about how I do things and like them to be done properly ☐

9 When discussing things, I put forward ideas that I know will work. ☐

10 I don't usually take things for granted and like to check
   them myself. ☐

11 I love information – the more there is to sift through the better. ☐

12 I'm usually the life and soul of the party. ☐

13 I tend not to jump to conclusions too quickly. ☐

14 I prefer to respond to things in a spontaneous, flexible
   way rather than to plan things in advance. ☐

15 I make decisions carefully after considering all the
   possibilities first. ☐

16 It's best to look before you leap. ☐

17 Rules and plans are boring and take all the fun away. ☐

18 More often than not, rules are there to be broken. ☐

19 I can often see better, more practical ways to get things done. ☐

20 I always take care to work things out properly. ☐

21 In discussions I often find I am the one keeping people to
   the point and avoiding wild speculation. ☐

22 When things go wrong I shrug it off and put it down
   to experience. ☐

23 It's best to think carefully before taking action. ☐

24 Quite often I figure out simpler, more logical ways to do things. ☐

25 It's silly to make a decision just because it 'feels right'.
   You have to consider the facts. ☐

26 I like to be absolutely correct about things. ☐

27 I prefer solving problems step-by-step rather than guessing. ☐

28 The most important thing about what you learn is if it works
   in practice. ☐

29 I prefer mulling possible outcomes before coming to my
own conclusion. ☐

30 I tend to judge other people's ideas on how well they will
work in practice. ☐

31 I come up with unusual ideas in discussions. ☐

32 I look at problems from as many angles as possible before
starting to solve them. ☐

33 Usually I talk more than I listen. ☐

34 If a thing is worth doing, it's worth doing properly. ☐

35 I believe that careful, logical thinking is the key to
getting things sorted. ☐

36 I like to consider all my options before making up my mind. ☐

37 It doesn't matter how you do something so long as it works. ☐

38 I do whatever I need to do to get the job done. ☐

39 I like meetings or discussions to follow a pattern and timetable. ☐

40 I don't mind in the least if things get out of hand. ☐

SCORING

Give yourself one point for every statement from 1 to 40 that you agreed with.
For example, if you put a tick against the first statement, put 1 next to the
number 1. Each answer is allocated a letter – an A, a P, an R or a T. At the end,
add up the score for each letter.

1. .... A	11. .... T	21. .... R	31. .... A
2. .... P	12. .... A	22. .... A	32. .... T
3. .... R	13. .... R	23. .... T	33. .... A
4. .... A	14. .... A	24. .... R	34. .... P
5. .... P	15. .... T	25. .... T	35. .... P
6. .... T	16. .... T	26. .... P	36. .... T
7. .... P	17. .... R	27. .... P	37. .... A
8. .... P	18. .... A	28. .... R	38. .... R
9. .... R	19. .... R	29. .... T	39. .... P
10. .... P	20. .... T	30. .... R	40. .... A

Write your scores down here.

My total score for: A .... P .... R .... T ....

Each letter represents a different learning style. The letters that have the greatest number of points represent your preferred learning style (or styles). So which one are you?

A is for ACTIVIST
Your motto: 'I'll try anything once.'

There's nothing you like better than getting stuck into things. You enjoy challenges, and you are always looking for the next thing to do. You are open-minded, outgoing and like to be the centre of attention. You prefer not to spend too long planning anything, and are good in a crisis. You like to motivate others.

Things activists should think about:
- You might prefer learning by getting on with the job in hand, so flexible, practical or activity-based learning might suit you particularly well.
- If you hope to go to college, remember that you might learn best through practical projects and discussion groups. You like immediate results, so see if your learning can be broken into manageable bites to keep yourself motivated.

P is for PLANNER
Your motto: 'If it's logical, it's good.'

You have a careful, logical approach to life. You like to question almost every-thing and usually enjoy solving complicated problems. You are something of a perfectionist and are happy being left to get on with things, though you like to have all you need organized before you begin a project. You may frequently ask questions like: 'Does it make sense?' or 'How does this fit with that?' You like certainty and may be uncomfortable when people make wild guesses or don't take ideas seriously.

Things planners should think about:

■ You are probably a natural learner and will be happy to continue studying in an academic setting. You will benefit from theory-based courses, experienced trainers and reading well-written books and articles.

■ If you want to get qualifications at work, you might enjoy learning with correspondence and evening classes. You will probably like the research side of some NVQs.

R is for REALIST
Your motto: 'If it works, it's good.'

You are highly motivated and down-to-earth. You like new ideas and are keen to see them work in practice. Realists need lots of information, see connections and are inventive. You tend to be impatient with people who can't make up their minds, and you don't much like open-ended discussions. You will be particularly attracted to working on real-life projects, and you appreciate the help of someone who can give you some valuable feedback and coaching.

Things realists should think about:

■ You probably don't mind sitting in classrooms, but you also like to be hands on, so it might be worth seeking out learning that involves plenty of practical exercises, such as a Modern Apprenticeship, where what you learn is directly useful and relevant to your job.

■ If you want to go to university, think about learning that allows a mixture of practical experience and theory.

T is for THINKER
Your motto: 'I need time to think about it.'

You are thoughtful, tolerant and generally unruffled, and you don't like to be rushed. You like to reflect on all possible angles carefully before you wade in to tackle a project. You prefer to adopt a low profile and you tend to be fairly quiet, but this does not mean that you do not have good ideas. Indeed, you often get to the heart of the matter by listening to others, taking their ideas on board and coming up with considered solutions.

Things thinkers should think about:

■ If you want to get qualifications at work, you might do best learning at your own pace. Taking the time to survey all the possibilities and choosing the right vocational course is just your style.

■ You are usually happy in the classroom, but you do like projects and practical experience, so if you want to go to college, you'll prefer learning that mixes theory with practice.

Help! I've got high scores in two or more styles

If you have similar scores in two or more groups it means you are equally comfortable with different ways of dealing with new information. We all learn things in a variety of ways – but most people have stronger leanings one way or another.

It's sometimes good for us to pick learning activities outside our normal style – it helps keep our minds sharp. For example, if you prefer to work alone, do so, but keep in touch with your mates.

■ Work matters to us

Making employment choices has been likened to sitting in a swivel chair in a circular room full of doors. Your job is to keep turning round, getting out of the chair and checking out what is beyond as many of those doors as possible. Some may already be partly open, others may be heavier to push. Unless you go through some of them and take a peek, you will never see what you could be doing on the other side. But, equally, this is about your future, so nobody should be pressurizing you to go through a particular career door if you don't like the look of it.

Remember, work is going to play a big part in your life. Here's what one government minister had to say about it recently: 'Work engages our ambitions and expectations; it helps to shape our identity and status. At its best, people find in their work not only fair pay for their efforts, but huge satisfaction in working with others and in a job well done ... Whatever our individual experience, work occupies a very large part of our lives: it matters to us.'

And that just about sums it up. The decisions you'll take over the next few years will make a big difference to your life. So keep an open mind, gather as much information as you can, work out whether you're really suited to higher education or whether you'd be better off studying part time or training on the job. If the choices you make are based on solid foundations you're far more likely to stay the course and achieve your goals. Be honest with yourself about what you're capable of and what you want, and you'll dramatically improve your chances of getting where you want to be and really enjoying your working life.

▓ Key points

- ▪ Allow yourself plenty of time to make your choices.
- ▪ Make sure you understand how much work different exam subjects and courses involve before you sign up for them.
- ▪ Don't feel pressured into going to university if you feel that vocational or on-the-job training might suit you better.

'Success is that
old ABC – ability,
breaks and courage.'

Charles Luckman

Chapter 12
Working smart

In this chapter you will find:

❏ Why you will always need to manage your own career

❏ That it's important to learn to network, and what a mentor can do for you

❏ Why you need to know your rights at work

❏ How work can damage your health

❏ What you can learn from your parents' experience

Work is different from school or college. Of course, you already know that, but have you ever thought about what the differences actually are?

The biggest one might surprise you. Schools and colleges are places that exist with the sole purpose of helping you. The staff are hired and paid to do whatever they can to enable you to acquire the skills and knowledge that you need to develop into a reasonably well-adjusted adult, and – very importantly – to pass your exams.

For a start, your boss is not paid to help you. Admittedly, looking after staff is part of the job – but he or she has other things to worry about first. If you do turn out to be fantastic at your job, a sensible employer will value you and may develop your skills and promote you – but only if it fits in with his or her business plan and the current objectives of the organization. At the risk of sounding cynical, it's an unusual manager who will put your interests before their own. So if you're hoping to find a boss who will work as hard as your teachers are doing right now to help you fulfil your potential, you are likely to be disappointed.

Even if you find a boss who takes a serious interest in training and developing you, the chances are you will only be working for him or her for a year or two before one of you moves on to a different job. That is what is so different from how it was in your grandparents' time. When they were the age you are now, it was not unusual to consider spending your working life with the same employer. Young people started as juniors at the bottom of the company ladder and worked their way up until they reached the limit of their capabilities or – as most women did at that time – left work to marry and bring up children.

Now if you want higher pay and more status you have to move from one organization to another. Job security has all but disappeared as companies buy and sell each other, merge, restructure, upsize, downsize, flourish and collapse.

All this is not necessarily bad news. There's a lot to be said for the freedom that a fluid job market offers to employees. But it does mean that you need to take responsibility for your own career. Managing your working life is something you need to learn how to do. You're already making a start by reading this book.

Starting the new job

There's little to match the excitement of beating other good candidates and landing a job you particularly wanted. Actually making a go of it, however, is something else entirely. Once the initial euphoria has worn off, the real work starts. Impressions do count and the impact you make in the first few weeks may be vital in sealing your longer-term success with that organization. (Much of this advice, by the way, also holds good if you are about to start a temporary or holiday job.)

Careful planning will pay dividends and help you to cope with any new-job nerves. Before your first day at work, ensure you have up-to-date information on the firm and what will be required of you. Think about asking for a quick tour before you start, so you will know your way around on the first day.

Remember to do all you can to build up good relationships within your team. The people around you are your key to getting established. Find out which of them seem especially happy to pass on knowledge and alert you to any pitfalls. At first, you are bound to make mistakes through no fault of your own and these can probably be easily corrected.

Get to know your work team

Don't forget that working in a team is a two-way process and even as a new-comer there may be various ways you can support others. This early network may prove more useful than you ever expected if you later progress with the same firm. You may even be allocated a mentor – someone with lots of experience who can help you as you get established (read on for more information about mentors).

Make sure that you understand what your department or part of the company is expected to achieve – and, if it is profit-making, what actually makes money. You don't want to discover later that you have been concentrating on tasks that your boss or organization do not consider important. Having clear targets early on can save you time and make things less frustrating.

If you do have concerns about any aspects of your work, it's always advisable to talk things over straight away with your immediate superior. It's easier to sort out potential problems early on rather than wait until crisis point.

In larger organizations, it's always worth trying to work out who is responsible for what. Senior managers may not wish to get involved in day-to-day details – there might be someone else better equipped to help you when you get stuck. It's a waste of your time if you have to spend ages trying to find something out for yourself. If you want to avoid constantly having to ask questions, one approach is to make a note of the things you need to know. Then decide who can best help you with your list. When you approach this person, ask when is the most convenient time of day for you to spend a few minutes together.

Where possible, try to carefully plan your tasks for the day or the week ahead. This approach should not only help you to meet deadlines, but should also give you ammunition if you feel the work goals being set by your boss are impossible for you to meet. Falling at the first hurdle is not the picture you want to present.

▩ Welcome to your zig-zag career

The best way to climb a cliff isn't necessarily in a straight line – you might have to go sideways in different directions. People's working lives are increasingly jumping around in the same way. This is what is sometimes termed 'having a zig-zag career'. By the time you are thinking about retirement, you will proba-bly have several careers to look back on. Hopefully, some of the best moves you make will be from personal choice as you keep learning and manage to leapfrog from one opportunity to the next. Yet other moves you make will be through sheer necessity.

For example, let's say you get a job in admin with a local company. You do well and eventually find yourself managing ten people. But you are over-looked for a promotion you wanted and realize you are bored with the work, which no longer stretches you. On a whim, you answer an advert and make a move to a much larger company. But it's far from an impressive-sounding job and the pay works out less once your transport costs are taken into account. At the new firm you are responsible for no one but yourself. Friends wonder if you have taken a step back. The work is also far more technical and you have to ask for lots of help. But your projects are completed so well you soon get promotion. You choose to make a series of sideways moves within the same company to broaden your experience – including two spells working abroad. Then, having had a great run for several years, disaster strikes. Your firm announces redundancies – and your job is among those being chopped. However, the redundancy money gives you a breathing space and you take a couple of months off. Fortunately, out of the blue, you run into a former client who knows your work and offers you a job on the strength of something you did for her years ago. And so it goes on ...

The lessons here are that changing or even losing your role can help you find a new direction. Over the years, you may resign from one or more jobs or be laid off. You will probably have promotions and lots of different job titles, and work for many different bosses, good and bad alike. People might work for you. It will all be part of your career journey.

▓ Time to network

If the idea of actively managing your career and jumping in and out of several different jobs over your working life appeals to you, you'll need to master a very important skill – networking. It's not difficult and it's all about finding and getting to know people who can help you succeed in the career area you're aiming for. That doesn't mean there's no point networking if you haven't decided what sort of work you want to do yet. In fact, networking can be a really useful way of finding out more about different jobs.

Networking is something you will do to one degree or another throughout your entire life. And the good news is that you already know how to do it. Making friends at school and getting to know other people through them is something you've been doing for years without even thinking about it. And you've got other networks too – family, relations, family friends, neighbours, work colleagues of your parents, teachers, careers advisers, and so on.

By this stage in your life you already know a lot of people and the trick to networking effectively is to start thinking about who they are and what they do outside the role in which you know them best. For example, your friend's mum: what does she do for a living? Where does she work and who does she work with? Did she go to university? If so, where, and which course did she do? If you think about her in that way you begin to see that she's more than just your mate's mum. In fact, she's someone who could be worth having a chat with because she might have useful information and contacts.

▓ It's not who *you* know – it's who *they* know

The other important thing to remember about networking is that it can lead you in unexpected directions. Let's say you are good with IT and want to do some work experience in an office. Your uncle has a business, so you ask him. He can't help, but he just happens to be a member of the local chamber of commerce and asks around. It then turns out your timing was immaculate, because an estate agent in town is desperate to find someone to put in a few hours every week sorting out the customer database. Hey presto – you not only have a part-time job, but a new contact for your collection.

Networks are informal and operate on the basis of give and take. You ask someone for help or information and later you return the favour if they need something. Because you are not working yet, you will find you are not in a position to return many favours. But don't worry about that – adults know it's one of the advantages of being a teenager.

However, a word of warning about CVs and networking. If you do want to approach someone in an organization who's been recommended to you as a possible source of work, think carefully before you send them your CV – unless they have asked for it. The reason for this is that sending them your CV immediately brands you as a job-seeker. If they are not actively looking for someone to hire they may be reluctant to see you – and a potential contact has been wasted. If you just send them a letter asking for a chat so that you can learn more about their company or sector, then they may feel more inclined to see you.

▓ Making contacts

Some people are natural networkers – the rest of us have to work at it. It takes courage to, say, walk into a room full of strangers and start up a conversation with someone. But inevitably one chat will lead to another – and the more you try it, the easier it becomes. Learning how to talk naturally to people you've only just met is a really valuable workplace skill. If you feel that you don't have it now, then work on it.

Here are a few basic tactics you could try out the next time you go along to a careers fair or you're sitting in a waiting room for a university interview with a bunch of other candidates.

- Pick a person you like the look of.
- Make eye contact.
- Smile.
- Ask them a question about themselves. (Where are they from? Have they been waiting long? Have they been to this event/place before? What do they think of it so far? It doesn't really matter what you ask – anything that gets the conversational ball rolling will do.)
- If they respond positively, introduce yourself.
- Relax and don't fall into the trap of thinking that other people are automatically judging you critically.
- Encourage the other person to talk about themselves but drop in the odd bit of information about yourself too or they'll feel as if they're being interrogated.
- If the conversation goes well and you feel you've made a connection, suggest you exchange email addresses (people are generally happier to give out their email address than phone number to someone they've just met).
- If you're getting nowhere, politely excuse yourself and move on.

Keep in touch

If you want to be really organized, why not try creating a database of the people you know and the skills, knowledge and experience they have? Typing out a list of names, attributes and contact details for everyone you know might seem a bit over the top but it does give you a good idea of the help you can call on – and you can build on it over time.

As time goes by, do keep in touch with your former contacts, teachers, bosses and colleagues, and keep a note of how and when you do so. Email or instant messaging on the internet makes this a relatively simple task. Make sure your files are always bang-up-to-date as people you know move into different roles, and keep your network informed about what you are doing.

Remember, many jobs are filled through word-of-mouth. Employers – especially the smaller ones – find putting the word out is one of the easiest and cheapest methods of recruitment. The more people who know what you're doing and where you're trying to go, the more likely your name is to come up when a good opportunity becomes available.

■ Look for a mentor

Sometimes networking can help you in an unexpected way by providing you with a mentor. A mentor is someone outside your family, school or immediate circle who can act as an independent and trusted guide and adviser. Mentors are increasingly popular at work, acting as sounding boards to help people become more effective or to help them decide what they want to do next.

This is an idea to keep in mind throughout your career. It's particularly useful when you're just starting out, but it's also something to think about at all stages, especially when moving on to a new role or field. Many senior executives rely heavily on mentors to keep their perspective on their work fresh, and some (usually large) employers offer a matching service where would-be 'mentees' are paired up with mentors from elsewhere in the organization.

There's no need to wait until you start work to make use of a mentor, and in many ways the sooner you find one the better. So how do you choose and recruit a mentor? Duncan Cheatle, founder of the advisory organization Prelude2business, reckons that if you possibly can you should find someone no more than about 10 years older than you to help you think through your career ideas. In this way, you are more likely to have someone to talk to who will not only inspire you but also still remember what it was like to be your age.

Think about everyone you know or admire and go for the best person you can. Just give them a ring – being young yourself can be an advantage when asking for someone's help. They feel flattered, and often genuinely want to put something back if they themselves have enjoyed early success. Many like nothing better than talking about their own experience.

▓ How mentors can help

Mentors can help you question your reasons for doing something, and can help you avoid learning lessons the hard way. They can dispel myths, give practical tips on applying for work or going for interviews, and help you make sense of your choices. Later, one could coach you in the workplace and perhaps shed light on the apparently strange or unpredictable behaviour of colleagues or managers you encounter – mentors have seen it all before.

According to Duncan Cheatle, entrepreneurs are often the best mentors for anyone as they are, by nature, free thinkers who question everything. They also tend to be better connected – just what you want if you are in the market for a little career guidance.

If you have no ideas where to find one, you could always try The Prince's Trust (aimed at young entrepreneurs) or networks such as Ecademy or Shell Live Wire. Another good tip is to look for local firms that have won entrepreneurial or community awards – they would probably be glad to speak to you. And don't worry about getting stuck with a mentor for life. If the relationship doesn't turn out well or you feel it's run its course, you can always bring it to an end with a polite thank-you letter and look for a new mentor. Over time you may even end up with several mentors, each equipped to help you with different aspects of your career.

▓ Know your rights

In the UK, the law protects workers from everything from discrimination and unfair dismissal to hazardous working conditions. It's there to help you, and we advise you to take a little time to find out about the legislation that governs your behaviour at work and that of your employer.

There are plenty of good books around on the subject, but you do need to keep your knowledge fresh because the law is changing fast in this area. The 'know your rights' area at www.tuc.org.uk is a good place to start. It will tell you everything you need to know and it's regularly updated.

You may be fortunate and never find yourself in a difficult situation at work. But if you do, you'll be much better placed to handle it if you know what your rights are and already have an idea of what to do.

So if the time ever comes when you feel you're not being treated fairly:

- Stay cool.
- Keep written, dated notes of everything that happens and everything that's said.
- Seek advice before you do, or say, anything rash.

If you've joined a trade union, it will be able to help you. Alternatively, you can drop in to your local Citizens' Advice Bureau for free, confidential guidance.

■ Work and health

As we've already set out in this book, how you choose to spend your working life will have implications for how and where you live and possibly even who you live with. It might also have implications for your health. According to the Health & Safety Executive, around 2.3 million people in the UK believe that either their current job or work they've done in the past has caused them to become ill or made an existing illness worse. The big problem areas are:

bone, joint and muscle problems
stress, depression and anxiety
breathing and lung problems

And the people most at risk of work-related illness or injury are:
police officers/armed forces/security guards etc
health and social welfare professionals, such as nurses
construction and building trades workers
teachers
research professionals
transport operatives
machine drivers
plant/machinery operatives
metal and electrical trades workers

Health & Safety Executive

■ How work can make you ill

Work-related stress has now reached epidemic levels in the UK and it's the most common reason (after back pain) why people need to take time off work or give up work altogether. So learning to recognize and manage the things that wind you up at work is likely to be an increasingly valuable skill. As you might imagine, certain jobs carry a higher risk of work-related mental illness (including stress) than others. A study for the Health & Safety Executive high-lighted people in the following jobs as being among those particularly at risk:

clerical

secretarial

administrative support

machine operators

social workers

industrial workers

sales people

teachers

nurses

police officers

probation officers

armed forces

medical practitioners

If research by Dr Peter McCarron is anything to go by, even your choice of degree could have implications for your life expectancy. His team followed up the health records of male students at Glasgow University over a 20-year period and discovered that science graduates tended to live longer than arts graduates.

- ■ Those who had studied arts subjects or law were the most likely to die young.
- ■ Divinity students had the lowest blood pressure.
- ■ Medical students were the heaviest smokers, followed by law students.
- ■ Science students were the least likely to smoke.

- Arts students were twice as likely as medical students to die of lung cancer, but half as likely to die from accident, suicide or violent means.
- Medics were the most likely to die from alcohol-related deaths.

Overall, medics were the least likely to die young, despite being the heaviest smokers at university (though the team reckoned that was because they were more likely to give up smoking in later life).

Don't allow work to make you ill

Most people never give a thought to the health implications of the work they choose to do, and the majority of people who earn a living in what are classi-fied as 'high-risk' jobs never have any problems. But if you are heading for a job like that it's worth keeping the risk in mind – you're far less likely to have an accident or develop a work-related illness if you're aware of the possibility and take steps to prevent problems before they happen.

Employers in Britain have a legal duty to take steps to minimize the risk of their staff being injured or becoming ill because of their work. If you feel your job is becoming hazardous to your physical or mental well-being, don't just put up with it. Arrange a formal meeting with your manager and ask for help.

Don't mix booze with business

Talking of health, time for a word about alcohol and work. Drinking often plays a large part in office and business life. But if you're smart you'll keep your working relationship with alcohol firmly under control.

Non-drinkers can find life tough at some companies where the pressure to drink with colleagues or customers can be intense. The tradition of drinks at particular times like Friday lunchtimes or after work can be firmly entrenched in a company's culture. Workmates and (even more awkwardly) bosses can be sur-prisingly hostile to the idea of you drinking orange juice while they get legless.

As you may discover when you start work, boozing is widespread among people doing high-pressure or repetitive jobs, and those involving a lot of client entertaining. The idea of being able to drink at your company's expense might sound appealing, but you should think about your relationship with alcohol and work before you get sucked too far into the drinking culture.

It does not stand to reason that just because others want to drink hard, so should you. Alcoholism kills more people in the UK than any other drug except tobacco, and one in every 13 adults is dependent on drink. Sleeping off your lunch every day in the stationery cupboard is not only a waste of time, it will also get you the sack. Employers don't want staff who can't handle alcohol sensibly – why would they, when a quarter of accidents at work are drink-related?

Bosses like staff they can rely on and heavy drinkers are notoriously unpredictable. Unpredictable behaviour impacts on colleagues and clients, and in the end drinkers usually find themselves out of work because they're just too risky to employ.

■ And a word about office parties

Office parties can range from a night out in the local pub to a formal black-tie dinner. Some are fun, others are boring, but they all can be a minefield for unwary new employees. We're including a little advice about them in this chapter because they can present you with an opportunity to do one of two things:

- ■ Spend an evening at your employer's expense.
- ■ Ruin your career prospects.

Behaving appropriately at office parties is simple and can be achieved easily enough by remembering one word: 'Don't'.

- ■ **Don't** dress strangely. (It's a mistake to think this is a chance to 'be yourself'. It isn't.)
- ■ **Don't** be drunk when you arrive.
- ■ **Don't** get (more than very slightly) drunk while you're there.
- ■ **Don't** tell your boss what you think of her or him (everyone does this at office parties – it's never a good idea although it always seems like one at the time).

- **Don't** tell your colleagues what you think of them (ditto).
- **Don't** criticize the venue, the food or the entertainment (someone has spent all year arranging your party and the chances are it's the person you're talking to).
- **Don't** tell anyone you love them (unless you're married to them).
- **Don't** get naked (not even semi-naked).
- **Don't** get more physically intimate with anyone than you would if your parents were watching (this can be construed as 'gross misconduct' and can get you fired).
- **Don't** get into a fight (ditto).
- **Don't** be the last to leave (you'll look like a loser and damage your promotion prospects).

Smart people behave really well at office parties and enjoy themselves by encouraging their most irritating colleagues to behave badly instead.

■ Age and the workplace

When you start job-hunting, one of the problems you might run into is that some employers write you off because they think you're too young to do the job. The same thing happens at the other end of the age spectrum as well. And that's something worth thinking about, because you might find that you need to work for far longer than your parents will have to.

For example, sooner or later you will need to splash out on a car and a home. Then you will need to earn enough money to finance your retirement, your children's higher education and possibly long-term care for your relatives or yourself. Indeed, some experts are predicting that we might all have to work into our 70s to provide ourselves with a reasonably comfortable retirement.

What is also true is that almost everyone will be in the same boat. As the population ages, there should be a much-needed change of attitude to older people in the workplace. This will be an improvement on the current situation where some corporate recruiters think the ideal age for a top manager is between 35 and 40. According to their way of thinking, anyone not in that bracket is either too young or too old.

▦ Changing your work–life balance

Another benefit of a zig-zag career (see page 204) is that it can allow you to change your priorities and alter the balance between work and the rest of your life. For example, at 25 you might be quite happy to work long hours and actively focus on establishing your career. Later, you could expect to reap the rewards in terms of higher pay and good prospects.

But as time goes by, you might be more interested in flexible hours that allow you to pursue other interests rather than going for a job that paid the highest possible salary. There again, it might be the other way round – you might decide to work less when your kids are young and focus harder on your career when they are older.

Of course, all this depends on a range of jobs being available to people of all ages, and that's not the case now. Only half the men and women aged between 55 and 64 in England have jobs right now. Some of them don't want or need to work but others who desperately need to work can't find employers to take them on. Anti-ageism legislation should change that in future but attitudes need to change too before we see a real difference – and that could take a long time.

▦ Stuff your parents can teach you (even if they don't realize it)

One final thought here about parents. You might feel there's not much they can tell you about the particular job you're thinking of doing. But if you think they've got nothing useful to teach you about work in general, you're probably making a big mistake. Because they've probably been working for years, your parents have accumulated plenty of wisdom about everything from handling tricky relationships with colleagues to interview techniques or coping with setbacks like redundancy.

Many of the skills you need to get on at work are common to all jobs – whether it's manual labour or chairing a board of directors. Life at work is all about:

- ▦ Working in a team.
- ▦ Handling relationships with co-workers and bosses.
- ▦ Negotiating (everything from days off work to pay rises and promotions).

- Problem-solving (from minor day-to-day difficulties to major issues like staff cuts).
- Moving from job to job.
- Dealing with disappointments (jobs you don't get; promotions you're passed over for; work goals you fail to achieve; colleagues who let you down).

Over the years your parents and other family members have almost certainly experienced both success and failure – and seen their friends and co-workers through triumphs and disasters. More than you realize, they will understand how important human relationships are at work and how central they are to a happy life. If you can learn to interact well with the people you work with, you stand a good chance of enjoying your job. It's one way that work is very like school.

Even if your parents say they don't feel they can offer you much in the way of career advice, do make a point of talking to them about their own working lives, how they've handled them, the things they feel they've done well and the areas where they feel they've been less successful. You'll learn a lot.

Meet your personal career consultant – you

On the face of it, the workplace of the future seems like a highly pressurized, even daunting place. It's certainly true that there are fewer obvious 'career ladders' to climb than there were when your parents were at school. But the upside is that, increasingly, youth is no barrier, and if you love your job and you've got what it takes, you won't have to wait in line for years to get promotion.

Just remember that the only personnel or human resources adviser who is always going to look after your interests is you. You will need to work out for yourself when it's time to ask for more training, more responsibility or a pay rise. Only you will know when it's best to move on and take your experience elsewhere.

The message is clear – those workers who are the most adaptable and who market themselves most effectively will definitely have most options and can best position themselves for 21st-century success.

■ Conclusion

Picture an average office building. While many people seem to enjoy what they do, there's another group usually to be found lurking behind their desks killing time. Every day, they sit in front of their computers, drinking their coffee and daydreaming between phone calls – wishing they were doing something else. If only they knew what that something else actually was. They are the sort of people who put signs on the wall that say things like: 'Look Busy, Here Comes The Boss'.

Many people fall into their first job. Good opportunities for salary, promotion or travel open up – and they go with the flow. They do really well. Yet, after a few years, they still wish they had planned their career better. Was this where they really wanted to be? Where might they have ended up if they had given their job preferences a little more thought?

Others might have spent their twenties travelling, or prolonging their studies, or drifting from one firm to another in search of something they liked. They might all have showed terrific early promise, but while their mates were surging ahead, they somehow ended up in dead-end jobs.

It's never too late for anyone to discover the kind of job that might better suit them – and retrain. But the longer you wait to make a fresh start the harder it can be, and it's tough to start at the bottom of a new career ladder when you've already taken on financial commitments like a mortgage or car payments or had a family. So think ahead and plan for what you want to do with your life now. You won't regret it.

'I don't think of work as work and play as play. It's all living.'
Sir Richard Branson

Further information

There are many hundreds of websites you can visit for more information about careers, courses, education, training, testing and numerous other work-related subjects.

Here, to get you started, are some of the most helpful ones. These addresses were correct at the time of going to press, but you might find a few of them no longer take you exactly where you want to go.

Your careers centre or library should be able to help with further up-to-date information – but don't forget you can find out a great deal about most subjects simply by using a search engine such as Google.

Note that neither the authors nor the publishers are responsible for the content or accuracy of any information contained on any websites listed.

▮ Connexions
General information – use to track down your local careers service:
www.connexions.gov.uk
Careers and course details – earn reward points for learning and work-based training: **www.connexionscard.com**
Help and advice on a wide range of educational, careers and personal issues:
www.connexions-direct.com

▓ Options and subject choices

Helpful information and links for each stage from primary school to adult learning: **www.bbc.co.uk/schools**

Site aimed at parents – everything from options to vocational education: **www.parentcentre.gov.uk**

▓ Qualifications

All you need to know about qualifications for schools and colleges: **www.dfes.gov.uk/qualifications**

▓ Further education and vocational training

Comprehensive starting point for researching education, training, lifelong learning and career planning: **www.support4learning.org.uk**

Government network of online learning and information services: **www.learndirect.co.uk**

Central site for Modern Apprenticeships in England: **www.realworkrealpay.co.uk**

Modern Apprenticeships in Scotland: **www.modernapprenticeships.com**

Modern Apprenticeships in Wales: **www.beskilled.net and www.elwa.org.uk**

Modern Apprenticeships in Northern Ireland: **www.delni.gov.uk**

Leading provider of vocational qualifications: **www.city-and-guilds.co.uk**

▓ Higher education

Search, apply and track full-time undergraduate courses in the UK: **www.ucas.co.uk**

Official graduate careers website – lists 1,500 employers and their vacancies: **www.prospects.ac.uk**

The Big Guide – what you need to know about applying to university or college: **www.ucas.ac.uk**

■ Career research

A fun source of help and guidance on the web: **www.fast-tomato.com**

Comprehensive advice on everything from choosing a job to writing your CV:
www.bbc.co.uk/radio1/onelife/work

An easy-to-use list of career-related web links: **www.careers.lon.ac.uk/links**

A–Z listing of career resources – with website ratings:
www.hintsonline.co.uk/surfing-your-career.htm

■ Self-testing and assessment

Online personality test – with career suggestions and information:
www.channel4.com/brilliantcareers

Assess your talents, values, interests, etc., and match to potential careers:
www.careerkey.org

Jobs enjoyed by different personality types (see Chapter 3):
www.doi.gov/octc/typescar.html

Links to various online psychometric tests and useful background:
www.computing.co.uk/Careers/Features/Psychometrics/online.jsp

Huge, innovative US site – sifts through 950 occupations to find those that
match your skills: **http://online.onetcenter.org**

Free US online assessments of values, careers interest, competencies and work
personality: **www.testingroom.com**

Professional developer of tests, plus useful information: **www.psytech.co.uk**

■ Additional help

Choices and challenges for young disabled people: **www.after16.org.uk**

Your rights under the disability discrimination laws: **www.disability.gov.uk**

■ Studying or working abroad

UK National Resource Centre for International Careers Information:
www.careerseurope.co.uk

Explore working and studying abroad: **www.prospects.ac.uk/links/Abroad**

The voluntary sector

Working for a charity: **www.wfac.org.uk**

Encyclopedia of charities: **www.charitychoice.co.uk**

National charities database: **www.charitiesdirect.com**

Public sector

Leading public-sector employment site with comprehensive link section:
www.jobsgopublic.com

Help for graduates who want to work in the public sector:
www.getalife.org.uk

Entrepreneurship

Advice for 16- to 30-year-olds interested in starting a business:
www.shell-livewire.org

Wide-ranging information on all aspects of small business:
www.businesslink.gov.uk

Help for young people wanting to overcome barriers and start businesses:
www.princes-trust.org.uk

Advice, consultancy and support for entrepreneurs:
www.prelude2business.com

Acknowledgements

The authors would like to thank:

Ann and Duncan for their unfailing support, and for never complaining about lost weekends, tasks left undone or authors' moods.

Ruth and Claire, for their valuable insights and practical suggestions, and Felix, for reminding us that there are more important things in life than work. Whatever they each end up doing, we hope they thoroughly enjoy it!

Our commissioning editor, Emma Shackleton, for her enthusiasm for our ideas, her practical encouragement and her reassuring faith in us from day one.

Our editor, Mari Roberts, for her sure-footed guidance, clarity of thought and uncanny ability to spot non-sequiturs and woolly thinking.

And Angela McMahon, for casting her highly educated eye over the manuscript, and for being the kind of careers adviser everyone needs but rarely gets.

More essential guides available in the Personal Development series from BBC Books:

Get Up and Do It!: Essential Steps
to Achieving Your Goals
Beechy and Josephine Colclough
Publication date: March 2004
ISBN: 0563 48765 8
CD ISBN: 0563 52346 8

Starting Out: Essential Steps
to Your Dream Career
Philippa Lamb and Nigel Cassidy
Publication date: August 2004
ISBN: 0563 52140 6
CD ISBN: 0563 52389 1

The Confidence Plan: Essential Steps
to A New You
Sarah Litvinoff
Publication date: March 2004
ISBN: 0563 48763 1
CD ISBN: 0563 52336 0

Agree to Win: Essential Steps
to Win in Your Work and Life
Hugh Willbourn
Publication date: August 2004
ISBN: 0563 52148 1
CD ISBN: 0563 52394 8

Find the Balance: Essential Steps
to Fulfilment in Your Work and Life
Deborah Tom
Publication date: March 2004
ISBN: 0563 52138 4
CD ISBN: 0563 52341 7

Embracing Change: Essential Steps
to Make Your Future Today
Tony Buzan
Publication date: January 2005
ISBN: 0563 48762 3

All titles are available at good bookstores and online through the BBC shop at
www.bbcshop.com